DUNES REVIEW

DUNES REVIEW

VOLUME 28 ISSUE 2
FALL/WINTER 2024

CONTENTS

Land Acknowledgement

Dunes Review is published on the traditional lands of the Grand Traverse Band of Ottawa and Chippewa Indians. It is important to understand the long-standing history that has brought us to reside on the land, and to seek to understand our place within that history. We thank the Anishinaabe people for allowing us to be here today.

Cover Artist's Statement

My interest in the landscape genre comes from a desire to visually capture the sense of place—*genius loci*. The image should reveal the essence of a particular scene, whether painted *en plein air* or reconstructed in the studio. What makes a particular place alluring? My paintings, I feel, should reveal the beauty and mystery unique to the location.

The cover image, entitled *Tara Dove*, presents the tranquility of a lakeshore. The water is calm, the air still. I agree with classical pianist Hélène Grimaud when she writes, "Nature is the ultimate muse." Being in and surrounded by nature is where I connect with something larger than myself. My hope is that my images convey that encounter.

—Joan Gallagher Richmond

Editors' Notes

There seems no intelligent way to sum up in a measly little editorial comment a journal this full of voices. There is nothing for me to say that the pieces themselves don't say clearly and in richer language. Every tone of voice, every sort of story—private history, public history, imagined conversations, love, and longing—it's here. The process by which we met these voices, though, is mostly invisible to you, dear readers. I wish you could feel the grace with which writers correspond with us, the patience with which they field our suggestions. Our readers and editors are similarly generous with their time and imaginations. Twice a year the *Dunes Review* is a hive of minds doing their best to make something beautiful. It gives me hope. Plenty of people these days are articulating the importance of art in trying and turbulent times. It matters. I hope this issue gives you some sustenance for the coming year. Thank you, as always, for your patronage. It matters a very great deal.

— Teresa Scollon

What is it about looking up? What is it about the sky that invites us to turn our eyes upward when we seek clarity, whether it's in wistful uncertainty or lively expectation?

In the words of Nancy Squires, *night is beautiful—but long*. We could say it the other way too: night is long, but beautiful. Those moments of hope are at times interminable and magical. The haunting sense that things are better somewhere else, thankfully countered by the pull of the present and its beauties.

I recently read a news article touting a study that found a "preference for AI-generated poetry." And while I can appreciate the efficiency and usefulness of artificial intelligence in other spheres, I have to reject the premise that anything AI-generated could be considered poetry. In my view, poetry's greatest accomplishment is its emotional impact. Robots and machines can't feel; they can only imitate our reactions to stimuli. This issue is teeming with those stimuli: scenes and characters and images to evoke your feelings. To poke at your human-ness. Let them sink in, and then look up.

—Jennifer Yeatts

Nancy Squires
WAITING

The frost is on the stubble,
The ice is yet to come.
We wait for it to grip the pond again.
I've only seen it yet
In puddles on the pavement.

Night is beautiful—but long.
I wish I'd slept more soundly,
Deeply like the earth in winter
Curled in on itself, insensible
To what is happening above.

There is somewhere I go
In the sound of a choir, singing
mysteries woven of human voices
speaking to the dark—that place
Is real as any other. Now

If only it would snow
Maybe I could lay me down
To sleep, like bears and bulbs
Field mice and ambitions
At rest beneath the ever-present stars.

Zach Keali'i Murphy
THE LIMBO

The cicadas are extremely loud this summer, and so are my mother's outfits. The leopard print high heels, the oversized sunglasses, and the hat with the pink floral arrangement on its brim are some of the more understated pieces in her wardrobe.

"You don't hear about the sun when it's behind the clouds," she once told me as she put her beet-red lipstick on in the mirror.

My mother always looks so beautiful, even when she's sad. Every time she comes back from the Friday night Limbo parties at the bar down the block, her frown has dipped a little lower than before. It's amazing how spending time in the company of other people can make you feel lonelier.

A "Welcome Home" streamer for my father has been strung across our house's front window for a year now. It collects more dirt with each wind gust, and its shiny colors have faded. My mom keeps saying it's a pain to take down. But it's also a pain to leave it up. Maybe a tiny part of her is holding onto hope. A thin, dangling shred of hope.

When my father went overseas for his job as an underwater welder for cargo ships—whatever that means—my mother and I became a lot closer. She taught me how to cut my own hair and how to play softball. After my father didn't come home when he said he was going to, she taught me you can't trust people even when they look you in the eyes, and she taught me that promises can be shattered and stomped over like broken glass.

"If he was dead, we would have found out about it," she once said. "If he's alive, he's making a choice to not come back."

Sometimes I create imaginary scenarios in my head about why my father hasn't come home. Maybe he got roped into a plot to save the world. Or maybe the work has just taken longer than anticipated. Or maybe he told us it would be three years instead of three months and we just didn't remember. After a while, I run out of explanations.

My mother was never one to sugarcoat things. She didn't even put frosting on my birthday cake this year. "Frosting isn't good for you," she says as she lights a cigarette from one of the candles.

I blow out all thirteen of them, and we hear a car pull up on the street in front of our house. We get up to go look. An old man that neither of us recognizes gets out of the car and walks over to deliver a package to the neighbor across the street, gets back into the car, and takes off. My mother takes a drag from her cigarette and stares through the screen door. The sounds of the cicadas intensify.

Ellen Lord
PASSERINE II

> "Hope is the thing with feathers---
> that perches in the soul…"
>
> —Emily Dickinson

Winter was harder than most—or perhaps we say that every year.
Solitude battles with isolation, a harbinger for anguish and gloom.
How December opened its frozen maw for darkness to seep deep
and stay.

> snowbound
> hard to breathe
> into a low sky

But now it's early spring—one of those breezy-glimmer days when
snowmelt swells the marsh and peepers emerge to herald Eros in
a cacophony of song. I am surprised to see our Kingbirds have
returned to their owl-ravaged nest. I know it's the same pair—they
bring sticks and cottonwood fluff to that old window box under the
eaves. I watch them chirp and flit as sunshine sequin the aspens—

> forest bathing at dawn
> holding on —
> to a gnarled branch

I'd like to ask the poet—how hope survives after interludes of quiet
despair. I think she would tell me to watch those Kingbirds, how
they flew to safety after a raptor's dark feast—how they held on in
rough winds then returned to begin again.

> long blue evening
> owl perched in silence
> to prey

Leah Skay
WITH POETS, OVER TEA

I've reached a level of such intense grayness with being alive that I feel I must speak with Emily Dickinson or Sylvia Plath. Presumptuous of me to even imagine they'd like a conversation, but quiet rage recognizes deepness in a silent agreement, and I think they understand it more than most. I imagine a world where both women are alive at the same time, just for an afternoon, in the kitchen of a squat yellow farmhouse somewhere in Massachusetts. Emily sits by the window, enraptured with the telephone wires slicing trees in half, and Sylvia tries not to stare at the electric oven too hard. Their mouths are sewn closed simply with death, without the thread or the needles; the scattered papers on the bare table tell me more than their voices. I bring us empty tea cups from my grandmother's cupboard (where did I get them? this isn't her home) and suspend the belief that these women would never speak with me, because they would. They're not unattainable, not mythic in any way but their sadness, and they cannot see anyone but me. We're just women in a house, our favorite reclusion.

Sylvia asks first, through her stack of computer paper I gifted her upon her arrival from wherever-else. She asks if I am her kind of person.

I don't know what she means, but I think I do. "I hope so. I'm a writer, just like you."

She shakes her head, narrows her eyebrows and points at the text again. She asks what I wear, what falsity, what false teeth. She asks again, trusting me to do the work, if I am their kind of person.

Am I what? A master? Never a master. They're masters. I've heard a hundred praises and a dozen sighs when their names come up. I studied writing at college, something I think they'd understand but scoff at, and Emily and Sylvia write the syllabus on tragic feminine writers. I am the student, scrambling in their shadows to be another good female writer with something to say that hasn't been said. I'm sure she doesn't mean it like that. Am I blank? Am I malleable to the whims of myself and others? Am I missing pieces and stitch the holes closed? I have an autoimmune disease and a brain tumor, but I don't think she means that either because neither is going to kill me. The problem is, I don't know. Sometimes I think I'm everything I'm meant to be. Sometimes I sway to a cocaine line of apathy and brain rot. Sometimes though, more than anything else, I wonder if I made it all up in the first place. If I'm reading the book wrong or just reflecting myself onto words that aren't meant for me. That's the worst part of poetry, I think. It can mean whatever I need it to mean, like a beachside psychic speaking in statements just vague enough to be specific and specific enough to be vague. Some would argue that's the best part of poetry, but sometimes I just want to be told what to feel.

Emily pulls away from the window and shakes her head at me, smirking at Sylvia with a playful challenge. Tea sloshes from her cup and onto the paper, a sluggish apology in her eyes as she covers her lip so tea doesn't fall from her mouth.

Emily's voice is quieter in my mind, lighter, in the space of the silence between us. But her telepathic jeers and jokes are louder with light challenge. Emily claims she sees just as any other creature sees, as though her eyes are the eyes we all share. And Sylvia agrees, shrugging and nodding and turning at me to do the same. After all, we all have the same eyes, don't we, writers?

Emily and Sylvia settle back in their chairs and turn to me. We look alike. Long brown hair, plainly pretty, the perfect peasant with a mind you can see through our eyes. I don't have any poetry to my name, though. I've tried a million times. Middle school English curriculum indicated that listening to Frost talk about the woods would give me the key to unlocking the literary universe. You can't understand anything more than a poet understands it. There was a correct interpretation, a set of rules that rhymed and repeated, and only four primary subjects to choose from: nature, love, emotions, or society. All the great poets were already dead. You can't touch classics. So I thought it was cruel when they pushed the pen in front of us at nine in the morning on a Tuesday and told us to emulate the great poets for a grade. Under the crushing fluorescent lights, we wrote.

It was the first assignment that I'd ever gotten a C on. It's stupid, in retrospect, because what are grades in the grand scheme of things, but the feedback sits in my chest to this day: "Needs more emotion. Look at Whitman. Remember: poetry isn't just sentences!"

It was clear that there was a strategy to poetry. Something lofty and purposefully distant that itched at the skin of humanity, but only in this specific way ordained by the Delaware Department of Education. That was fine—I could handle patterns, but somehow the subjects were never *deep* enough. I got through it all fine, resigned to the fact that I could follow the rubric for the grade. And then college happened. The required Intro to Poetry course opened with the dreaded sentiment: "Throw everything school taught you about poetry out the window! There are no rules!" And then proceeded to still grade us, but that's beside the point. The prospect of having free rein ruined my strategy. What was I supposed to do? And perhaps even more dreaded was answering the question of why. Why did the author choose to write about this topic this way? Of all the ways to say it, why this?

Because they did. They're dead; they can't say anything more. This is all I had to work with.

I loathed every poetry class if only for having to listen to my peers recite their masterpieces. In my ear, they were all beautiful, terrible, and untouchable. It was a language spoken only to those who understood it immediately, and when it was my turn to give feedback, I found myself straddling the line between bitterness and awe. Most of the time I leaned into my enthusiasm to hide my discomfort. Now I wonder if I did myself a disservice. Those writers were fine without my input. I think my work has suffered for it.

I must be thinking too loudly because Sylvia scoots her chair into the center of the kitchen. She pulls up a loose tile and redness tinges her cheeks. I wave it away. She fingers the papers in her hands and places another in view.

Sylvia takes my hands in hers, rolling the skin across my fingers away from the bones like ripples in a lake. She leads my hands to her knees, then mine, and then stares through me.

I think I know this one.

Lady Lazarus. This poem always bothers me. It feels like reading her guts. Of course, that's why Sylvia wrote it. She wanted someone to see, even the invisible no one on the other side of the page. She always had her guts spilled out in front of everyone, and sometimes I think that's how she liked it. The first time she tried to kill herself she crawled under the porch and prayed that the blackness would hide her until she wasn't around to hear the criticisms. After every time she tried to die, she was dragged back into the facilities to polish her brain with electricity. My mother says that suicide is nothing more than the coward's way out, but I think Sylvia just kept screaming. Everyone has thought of killing themselves, passively or actively, and it's a black-or-white decision; kill yourself or swallow it all whole. Sylvia did both.

"No, we're not the same—" I protest, but Sylvia slaps my hands on her knees and back to my own. The skin on our bodies turns red with impact. I think she'll beat me with my own hands until I agree with her. Until I understand and believe that at the depths of somewhere undecided we are the same. She's almost crying now. I am too. The anger is infecting us both.

Emily rises from the table, half slouched, and waves me towards the back door. It shudders in the breeze, age wearing down the hinges so they whine as we open them. Sylvia stays back, and Emily and I are alone. She spins in the grass, skirts swallowing the dandelions beneath her, but there's a vacantness in her eyes. She flinches at the slightest bird, the car horns off in the distance, my breathing. She flops into the grass and invites me to join. She looks at me like she wants me to say something. Anything.

"Every time I read your stuff, I get annoyed."

Emily laughs, shrill and shocked by the looks of it, but she's silent. They're always silent.

"No—I'm not supposed to say that, I know—it's not a thing about your skill, or anything. Just seems like…you break everything. Like in school, we're taught to write this way or that way, and then they make us read your stuff and it's just…"

Between the bees humming in the flowers, the westward traffic, Sylvia's silent visage paces back and forth in the kitchen window. A nervousness that comes with fame, with publishing in your lifetime, with debuts and discussions and dead-eyed talks over tea, seeps out of Sylvia's pores like milk. But when I look at Emily, splayed out in the grass, eyes on the sky with her hand on her heart, the words of her mind appear in the sky, handwritten on letters that only some were supposed to read.

She writes that publishing, in all of its forms, is an auction for the intelligent and listless. We sell our work, leaving us poorer, and we march onward with our notebooks towards some deniable future layered in snow and rejection and so much else to take. Her cadence broken by sighs and smiles, the flicker of her attention elsewhere, Emily tells me that success is a type of death, one of the only types that matters.

"That feels counterintuitive though. Like, aren't we supposed to want to be published? To be read? If not, what's all the practice and the skill for? I'm not rich enough to write for fun. Or for work, for that matter. It's nice to do it for the art or whatever, but...I don't know. We can criticize it all we want but at the end of the day...we still sell our soul at auction, right?"

I can never find the words for Emily. I don't dislike her, but I don't like her either. Sometimes, I wonder if she's been warped into an established literary manic-pixie-dream-girl. Wild, uncaring, weird on purpose with a sort of privileged laziness that allows her to just be art. We don't make writers like that anymore. I wonder how much of her reputation comes from annoyed academic men of decades past deciding her persona for her. She was rough, emotional, sentimental in ways only people with a true, deep fear rooted in their chest can stomach. She was told her entire life that her destiny was to die, probably of tuberculosis or some other brutal disease. Maybe that's why she made such close friends with Death.

She capitalized Death when she wrote about it, so I feel as though I must too, to do her service. Death was her living muse, the object of her obsessions and perpetrator of her terrors. I don't write about Death much. Or Love. I feel like I can never get where I need to go, like no words in this language or any other can grasp the depth at which those concepts seep into me. The words just won't come out. I've come to understand that real writers write about the things that hurt, the heaviest weights of being alive, and that one must be tortured to make something worth reading. And reading these poems, contemplating the meaning of the individual words and hyphens as if Emily was a madwoman so obsessed that she threw all care for grammar aside, surrounded by a classroom of stuffily-dressed authoritarian academics, digs a hole in my optimism for the future of literature. It feels like we're missing the point. I don't know what the point is.

"Oh, and I hate your em-dashes. Are you why they call them that? Em—dashes? Never mind, that's stupid."

Back inside, Sylvia and Emily share a plate of butter cookies and farmer's market raspberry jam with their tea. They speak to each other in silence, feverishly sliding manuscripts and poems back and forth between the napkins. Eyes wide, enthusiastic nods, the women embody everything I'm supposed to feel. And I sit on the other side of the kitchen, my back against the cool blue wall, watching them through the film of a feeling I can't discern. It leaves a bad taste in my mouth, sour.

A sob threatens to rip my throat apart. My words echo heavy in the halls, through the stairwell, along the cobwebbed bedroom walls, out of the faucets, and into the soil.

"I feel like I'm failing at something that's impossible to fail at. Everything's been said. Everything's been done. There's nothing left to say or do. It's all just…you. And them. And everyone else. I don't get it. What am I missing?"

Emily's eyes say it all: *Don't you see? Don't you see?*

"I wish you could just talk to me. I have so many questions."

And we have no answers.

Emily writes about crumbling, about the slow cascade into it, the asking of questions and the lack of answers and the vitality of falling to nothing. Poets aren't scaffolders with mechanics and blueprints, but interpreters at the verge of falling apart at every turn. They're not sturdy, omniscient, or untouchable. They're people. They're artists. They're crumbling all the time.

I can feel it. Their eyes, their words, their secret, phenomenal presence behind the pages of my books. They're reaching for me. I reach back, touch the palms of their hands, and my fingerprints are slit as if their skins are made of diamonds. I want to understand them. I want to be understood *by* them. I want someone to look at me like I have the answers to some long-dead mythos when in truth, I just like the look of the graveyard. I don't mean to be selfish, but I mean to be proud.

And when I read them, when I sit in the house in Massachusetts with their ghosts, I am terrified that I am understanding their paintings and not their muses. They're not who I believe they are, and all of my questions filter through the panic of not being academic enough to be serious. The image of the greats is a fallacy: artists born as people, peasants in the world, warped by the minds and mouths of people who never knew them, and yet the Greats are the influential ones. They're the victims of their own intellect, passions, terrors, and pens. Sylvia was a woman with a sadness that touched her soul, she was crying for help and getting accolades for her suffering instead of therapy. Emily was an observant young noble that knew Death followed her as lazily as it followed any other, but couldn't shake its gaze. They were just people, idolized and altered. That's no service to them. It's no service to anyone.

And yet, I come to the table with cookies and jam, to listen to them speak at me and to take my notes as if somewhere through spacetime they'll teach me the secret to sitting at their table. It's bitter bile in the throat of creation itself. The point is moot. The point is out the window Emily can't stop staring through, burned in the oven with Sylvia's brain, and bubbling in the cold fury in my chest. This is my distinct rejection; I'm alone. I can talk to them all I want, but they can't teach me what I want to learn. I can feel them reach out for me, reminding me that they are nothing more than writers from another year. I am just another writer from another year. There's power in that. There's beauty in burying the dead.

Afternoon climbs on the house in Massachusetts. It's odd how so many American classics come from that little New England state, but that's a pointless jealousy to have now. I can't keep coming back here. There's always something to learn, but not until I can learn there's something beautiful in the misunderstanding, in the ego of creating something worthy and unworthy of holding, in the blip of existence where I hold a book and a mind speaks to me through time. The interpretation interrupts the imagination. I can't come back to this house until I'm ready to fix it up, clean it out, bring juice in plastic jugs because I can't stand tea. I can't lean on their greatness until I can lean on my own. Call it spite, call it arrogance, call it peace, call it whatever you want—I'll find the words for it later. But now, I leave the house in Massachusetts, and as I turn away from the kitchen towards the door, I can feel Emily and Sylvia smiling over my shoulder.

My organized decays seep into my stomach. I attend the public auction of my soul with every submission, ripping my mouth open from stitches self-sewn. My hands write words, my knees smack under the table as I pull my chair away from the wall to reach for a spare pen. I can see how every creature has longed to see, through generations of women writing words on paper with no idea what will become of it.

I am their sort of person.

Jared Pearce
BLUES

I'm waiting for the sky
to fix my eye and pull
the world into place.

Where's my Jesus
and his sussafruss of love,
unwinding Lazarus

to a fracas of blue light
that crinkles his new eyes
when he limps from the tomb,

or finding the shade of Mary's shawl
when she crawls to His cross,
the same as the sky he called?

And where's the air
my Love will share,
tone me on her wing,

pluck me in her beak
when she tweaks the shell
of day across the bed?

I'm listening for the blue
in you and me to be
that purity, at first weak

and wet, and then it wrings
itself free and sings and sails
out on the morning

in the sky of grace,
dropping now and then
to face the luscious worms

and veiled nuts,
to nest and know the husk
and meat of living.

Janice Zerfas
BLACKBERRIES

There are no blackberries in this poem.
Farther on in the yard where we target practiced,
weight of blackberries rise and vanish in deep briars.
Bits of swollen iron. The absolute purity of darkness.
They lean under blue-skulled weeds, nightshade retaking
interred yellow stars. But recall my claim, my reminder,
not one blackberry in this poem. Not one, though
they are delicious, growing wild, still there despite
the pre-solstice heat wave and accompanying drought.
Stuck in junipers too low for vultures,
and too far in to reach with a hand without dragging briars,
scratching, cutting a hem. Nor are there blackberries
down M-140 at the fruit stand, or local Costco.
You think aquifers replenish to feed your desire,
your wish for blackberries? To watch starlings
drunk on blackberries while the target practice stump
decanted to dirt. You are tempted to drive slowly,
hoping to spot a field's sweet spot, trespass.
This is no partial deal. Understand,
living and deceased, not one taste.
Walk all day in the back acre, but you will not
find one blackberry in this poem, on this tongue,
or you.

Calvin J. Maestro, Jr.
IN THE SUMMERTIME

It wasn't always like this. I had bought the up-north Michigan cabin decades ago when the kids were young. We'd spend the whole summer at the cabin camping, swimming, boating, fishing, hiking, and riding our bicycles. We'd keep warm all night long at the open fire pit looking at the sky. The stars and the planets would become visible shortly after dusk as the air was so pure and clear. I bought a professional telescope for the kids to look through. In little time, they became proficient amateur astronomers.

After I had used up all my vacation days at work, I would spend weekdays back home near Detroit and commute north during the summer weekends. My wife and kids would stay at the cabin and await my return. Every Friday I left work and drove up, only to return to Detroit early Monday morning. We became a close family. And we thought the good times would never end, especially after our kids had children of their own. My wife so adored her grandchildren.

After I retired from work, my wife and I sold the old home and moved to live full-time in the cabin. But then my wife became sick, very sick. And she died. I now was left alone in the cabin by the woods. The kids tried their best to visit whenever they could. But it wasn't the same. Soon, they started making excuses: their kids were sick, they had to work overtime, the children were at summer soccer camp, or the high school sports practices started earlier in the summer, etc. And gas was getting more and more expensive.

I managed all alone during the weekdays. It was the empty weekends that got to me, especially during the summer. I'd sit in the living room with a faded family photograph resting in my hand. It reminded me of the good times. The family picture was one of hundreds my wife had taken while our kids were growing up. She especially treasured the photos of our grandkids. But now, all her photograph albums collected dust while they sat on wooden bookshelves. It pained me too much to look at them.

And the photographs were not the only thing that was fading. It started with a "small fire." I had left something cooking on the gas stove and then forgot about it. Worse yet, I took a nap. The fireman told me that this was not unusual for people living alone. The fire damage wasn't too bad, but I had forgotten to renew our cabin's home insurance. I had thought everything had been switched to automated payments.

The house repairs took a big chunk of my life's savings. Then I fell and broke my hip. The workmen had left a few of their items lying on the floor and, as my eyes had inferior cataracts, I failed to spot the unexpected obstacles in my path. The doctors said this was a common cause of falls in the elderly. I was now a medical statistic. They first sent me to a rehabilitation center, then back home with home therapy, including scheduling a residential visit with a social service person.

The night before this social service person's visit, my hip started hurting, and I lost count of how many pain pills I took. The social service worker showed up bright and early the next morning, while I was still drowsy. It didn't help that I slurred my words and could barely answer her questions. She ended the interview by saying, "I understand."

A week later, my son, Joseph, showed up at the cabin—on a Monday of all days! "Dad," he said, "We need to talk." Apparently, it had been determined that it was too dangerous for me to remain home. Joseph then added, "People are coming to take you away in an ambulance, to Rest Heaven Adult Assistance Home." Who was he kidding? I knew it was a nursing home. "What if I don't want to go?" I said. My son looked at me. "That's why a policeman is coming along with a court order from a judge."

Initially, Joseph visited me in the nursing home once a month. Then once every three months. It has been 243 days since he last saw me. The nurses believe I haven't noticed his absence. They think I can't remember what day it is, let alone the month. Sometimes I mess with the staff's minds by stating the wrong date. Coincidentally, the dates I tell them are all famous times in history. But they never seem to catch on. I now spend my days sitting in a wheelchair in front of my room's window. I watch the birds flying free in the sky. I can also predict the passage of the sun as it moves across the top of my window throughout all four seasons.

As I sit in the wheelchair, all alone in the nursing home room, I hold in my hand the same old, faded family photograph I held decades ago when I lived in the cabin. It is the only photograph of my family to survive the move. I can no longer discern if the added fading is due to the photo itself or to my worsening eyesight. Memories are fading in my mind as well. Soon, all that will be left of my life will be that one photograph. If that at all.

Perhaps, as my last wish, they will let my corpse hold this old photograph just before they cremate me. It'll happen in the summertime, of course.

Onna Solomon
IN PRAISE OF MY GRANDMOTHER'S BODY

I don't remember the first time I heard my grandmother say it. Her directive is bound to my memory of padding down the carpeted hallway to the wood-paneled den where my grandparents sat in their matching recliners, waiting for me to model all my new school clothes. I picture myself at age eleven, thin-limbed and tall for my age, standing proudly in front of her in one of my just-purchased outfits. In all the years I visited them, I never had trouble finding clothes that fit in the standard-issue chain stores at the Midland Mall, where my grandma waited outside the dressing room, approving or discouraging choices I made from a bounty of possibilities. When we got back to the house, I would try on each piece of clothing, trotting out to them, spinning, delighted to be modeling for them—my prettiness, the look of me, clearly a joy to both of them. *You have such a nice figure*, she would say. *Don't get fat like me.*

It was something she said that I took as both obvious and irrelevant to me: a fact that didn't apply to me, someone whose body fit without effort. Growing up, it was a given that thinness was desirable, and so it was a phrase I heard my grandmother speak over and over that floated into the ether, a nearly invisible mote of dust in the atmosphere of How to Think About Bodies that I breathed in and exhaled without question. I can still see the two of them, Betty and Ben, sitting there in those big, cushioned chairs, beaming at me, taking me in—I felt treasured in a way I've never felt in any other relationship. The beloved granddaughter.

The family story about my grandmother's body was that it was beautiful until it wasn't. This story has been told all my life. It's the story she told about her body, that our family told: her fat body was bad and ending up with a body like hers was to be avoided at all costs. Her sister, my great aunt Lois, told stories about watching Betty, ten years older than her, getting ready for dates as a young woman: how after she put on her red lipstick, she would purse her lips, pull her cheeks in, and look at the angles of her face in the mirror. I couldn't take my eyes off her, Lois said, she was so glamorous, a tinge of mourning in her voice, like it was a personal loss to her that her sister's body grew and changed.

For the girls and women in my family, being told you look beautiful is a part of feeling loved. Being pretty (read: thin and feminine) and being adored go hand in hand in our mythology. When I was young, the elders would talk in quiet tones about the cousins or aunts who arrived to Thanksgiving in bigger bodies. I was never one of them. This is not a remarkable story—my family is not close to the worst of body shaming and food policing common in our culture—but it was clear from an early age that the easiest, least fraught path to adoration was to keep my body small.

❊ ❊ ❊

My grandmother's big, soft body was a delight and a comfort to me all through childhood. On visits to their house when I was very young, I would sleep with her and my grandpa in their California king bed. I would lay my head on my grandma's chest and stretch out sideways across the enormous mattress, pushing my feet into my grandpa's side, greedy to have her body all to myself. He would protest, This is my bed too! as I shoved at him, wishing him away so I could luxuriate in the bounty of her, the feel of my head on her ample bosom as I inhaled the floral scent her perfume—the sensory memory of it visceral for me still. Before we have conscious memory, we have sensory memory that is stored deep in our nervous systems. The feel and smell of my grandmother is fused with a feeling of safety and love in that deep unspeaking part of me.

It was not until I had my own kids and my own body began changing and growing, at times becoming incomprehensible to me, that my grandma's words began to hold more meaning: Don't get fat like me. Now in my forties, I observe my body, sometimes with tenderness, sometimes with disbelief, sometimes (I will admit) with shame and sadness: my softening belly, my thickening arms, my widening hips. I witness the comfort my kids get from laying their heads on my belly or chest, how they relish my softness. I think of her and I wish I could go back and tell her that this is what she was for me.

I don't know how much time my grandma spent thinking about her body, how much effort she spent trying to make herself smaller. My guess is that it was not a little. We never talked about that when she was alive, never addressed the cost of her belief that her body once had value and then lost value, that her body was some kind of cautionary tale, as if she had been careless with a precious gift and let it drop somewhere, never to be found. It didn't occur to me to be curious about it, so I never asked her. I never questioned this story about my grandmother's body until she was gone, and my own body continued to get bigger. I felt that I didn't have much control over how my body was changing, or at least I didn't feel it was worth the obsession it would take to assert control over it.

How do I hold onto the feelings of love and adoration that are so tied to those words—*Don't get fat like me*—as I rewrite the story of her body, and, in doing so, write a story about my own body that I can live with, that I can live by? That I can live in. I'm committed to revising the family story, so I inhabit my body in a way that my grandmother wasn't able to inhabit hers.

❖ ❖ ❖

My grandma was a master joke teller. Many of her jokes were bawdy, not to be told in mixed company, as she would say. One of her favorites was about a woman who was going in to have surgery and prayed, *Please, God, let me live.*

God told her, *Don't worry! You will live a long time.*

Well, in that case, she thought, *while I'm under the knife, I'll get my lips done, and a boob job, and a few other things fixed up.* She had her surgeries and recovered without any problem. When she walked out of the hospital, as she stepped off the curb, she was hit by a bus and died. When she reached heaven, she said to God, *What happened? You said I would live a long time!*

God said, *I didn't recognize you!*

I have a video of my grandma telling this joke. She is less than a year from death, sitting there laughing with her hand over her mouth, beautiful in the light of the shaded lamp beside her. The joke and my grandmother telling it, the look on her face and her ease, the intimacy of the moment, the lens from which I was recording, trying to hold on to what I had with her—all of it has layers of complexity that are hard to untangle. Watching this video, I am struck by the punchline, that even God cannot see past the way a woman's body looks. I am trying to understand how my grandma's love for me, her humor, her understanding of womanhood, is woven into to the ways my body is sometimes a barrier to my own joy.

There is an ache I feel when I wonder if the deep love of my grandparents was, even a little bit, predicated on my body fitting into their vision of the adored granddaughter: pretty and thin—in other words, easily acceptable by anyone's standards—someone they felt proud of looking at, of showing off to others. In order to allow myself to love my aging, growing body, I have to accept that one reason it is so hard is that I believe I will lose that uncomplicated feeling of adoration that came to me all those years my body was thin and young and easy to admire. And to accept that is to accept that my grandma's love was imperfect. Is it true that the feeling of being held and safe was dependent on my body being a certain way? I know my grandparents would never have said so. The family story of my body that has been told—or maybe it's more accurate to say the story of my body that I have told myself—is filled with images seen through their loving, assessing eyes. By changing the story of my grandmother's body, I also must question the story of how unconditional the love for my body actually has been, and that is a hard thing to allow.

※ ※ ※

My grandmother was fat for my entire childhood. She did not become thin again until she was shrunken by old age, her appetite subsiding, her muscles weakening and bones becoming frail. By then I was in my thirties and had just had my second child. I have a picture of her in her hospice bed, a deadpan look on her face, giving the photographer the middle finger. Her high cheekbones are prominent over hollowed-out cheeks. Her thick, salt-and-pepper hair is neatly combed and she's wearing red lipstick. The picture was taken weeks, maybe days, before her death.

When she was dying, the stories people told about her had little to do with her body. There were passing allusions to how beautiful she was as a young woman, and pauses after those comments filled with silence about what her body was for most of her adult life. But the truth is that my grandma's words—Don't get fat like me— were not nearly as powerful as her deeds. When I look back at the months leading to her death, it is clear to me that she modeled how to live a rich, meaningful, joyful life in a fat body. As she was dying, she had a steady stream of visitors—family, neighbors, the adult children of long-dead friends, and even workers from her independent living apartment building who paid visits to her in their off hours because they wanted to say goodbye. Cards from old friends too fragile to visit shared stories of how much they felt her love and care, how much she made them laugh, how witty she was, how she was a consummate cook and host.

My grandma was a source of luxurious comfort for me. The many moments I spent close to her body were moments of feeling wholly safe and loved and in full pleasure. It shocks me that it has taken me so long to recognize the dissonance in the story that was told to me and the story that has been true to my life. When I try to explain this to my mother, she doubles down on the family lore. She says that my grandmother's fatness caused her problems (knee pain the only one she can really name, because my grandma's health was actually pretty good overall—she could hear a whisper in another room, barely took any medications, and died at age ninety-three). She says, I was with her when doctors told her she should lose weight. I tell her she is missing my point, which is that somehow, we have all agreed to believe that the whole of what a woman's body contributes, the whole of how my grandma's body served her life, of what value it had, was, ironically, diminished by its size.

What I am trying to say is this: the story that continues to live in the deepest parts of me is that my grandmother's body was glorious, was delightful in its fatness, its softness. All the memories of her, all her goodness and humor, are, for me, tied to her body just the way it was, not in spite of it. Whatever other truths there are about my grandma's body, and there are many—the truth of how her family saw her, how her doctors explained her health, how she saw herself—there is the truth of how her body is inextricably linked to her love for me and my love for her. That the truth of her body just as it was, plump and perfumed and radiating affection for me, gave me a kind of love I have never had in any other relationship and never will have again. And how can that truth be any less important than all the others? As I sort this out, I sometimes feel sad and angry that I did not fully understand this until after she died, because I wish I could have shared this with her, though I'm not sure I would be able to get her to understand.

Genevieve Betts
MY MIDDLE-AGED BODY

I love my middle-aged body
because it is finally all mine,

not my childhood body under
the control and style of adults,

mom-created hairdos yanked
too tight against my scalp,

or my teenage body, verboten
of a loss of virginity, as if some-

thing of value, like an antique
ruby-dotted ring, would be stolen,

sold in some pawn shop, seedy
and tucked into a roadside plaza,

not my adult woman body, creating
and feeding other humans like any

mammal does, an animal decade
of colic and milktooth. Since then,

I have measured out my life with
birth control pills, menstrual cycles,

the graying of hair against each
temple, a funny word to describe

the rounded corners of my braincase.
And if the body is a temple, let mine

house the sacredness of my mind,
its gardens and toads, imaginary,

real, or otherwise, and all that I've
planted there, heirloom and vibrant.

Bryan Gruley
THE GATORS OF NORTHERN MICHIGAN

My gold mine is hole number ten at Splendid Acres Golf Course, just off M-72 not far from Kalkaska. A pair of ponds ringed by weeds and cattails squat on opposite sides of a narrow ramp of fairway leading to the green. Beckoning the hapless golfers.

From my hiding place in the oaks and elms and scrub beyond the ponds, I hear the hackers yakking and smacking their lips on the tenth tee. They're about to whack their four-dollar-and-fifty-cent balls into vacuums. And late that night, when they're all hooting drunk on Bud Light and Fireball at the Kal-Ho or the Hide-A-Way or their rentals on Bear or Starvation or Big Twin, I'll strap a mask and infrared lamp to my head, pull on my flippers, and slip into those ponds with a fishnet sack that'll hold enough Titleists and Bridgestones, Callaways and TaylorMades to fetch me three or four hundred bucks on the deep, dark market for poorly struck golf balls.

That honks Wantje off. He runs the golf course. In his mind those balls are his balls, his property, his money. He paid off the county fathers—all fathers, no mothers--to make it illegal to ply my honest trade. Who does that help? Nobody. Not me, not the driving ranges that buy my barely used balls, not the cops who give zero damns about my harmless pursuit, not the county, not even Wantje himself. Not a chance he's wading into a soup of leeches and snapping turtles and pesticides that'll fry your eyes.

Wantje probably thinks he's the good guy and I'm the villain, but really he's just that Caddyshack groundskeeper in a pricey golf shirt he probably didn't pay for and I'm the innocent varmint trying to fill my belly. For Christ's sake, we're talking about golf balls here, not good and evil. To hell with useless rules made up by lazy losers like Wantje who don't want to do the dirty work. I do the dirty work. Kicking down through the green murk, my headlamp ablaze, I see the balls glowing like jewels in the sludge. A corroded pipe runs through a rut at the bottom of one of the ponds, an old irrigation line or something, and balls seem to propagate there like eggs from a chicken. Sometimes I spend my entire night scoping and scooping beneath that blessed pipe.

Wantje's been conniving for three years to catch me in the act. Almost succeeded a couple of times. Usually, I can sneak into one pond and scoop up enough balls to make the night worthwhile. Takes me barely an hour of diving and coming up for air and diving down again. Unless Wantje stakes me out at the crack of midnight, sitting between the ponds in a lawn chair with a spotlight, he's no more likely to see me than he would an alligator lumbering across the fairway like we were in southern Florida, not northern Michigan.

Once Wantje was out there, standing with a twelve-gauge on his shoulder. I could tell he was in his cups—everyone knows Wantje loves his double-Captain-and-cokes—and I probably could have pulled off a little larceny right in front of his eyes, but I didn't want to chance a shotgun in his shaky hands. I snuck back through the woods to my truck and headed over to Twin Birch, hole number sixteen with that shallow, snaky, hard-to-see creek in the middle of the fairway. I gathered myself an acceptable haul and celebrated with a Stroh's, maybe two or three.

Wantje has gone to the extent of hiring lawyers, including a fancy one out of Traverse City who sent me emails and letters and, eventually, a certified letter I had to sign for, all ordering me to cease and desist from plundering the ponds at Splendid Acres or they'd prosecute to the fullest extent of the law. I didn't know there was a law about balls that golfers unintentionally hit into ponds and then intentionally leave behind. If anything, the golfers owned those errant balls, not Wantje or Splendid Acres, and if they wanted them back, all they had to do was come to my two-bedroom on Crooked Lake and ask. I'm pretty sure Rock-O, my pit bull, would leave them be. (You need a trusty guard dog if you have a shed where you clean and de-grease all those balls.) What I would tell my wife, if I still had one, is that I may live in the muck, but I am not a thief. No, sir. I provide a service.

Speaking of alligators, a week or two ago I heard some regular at Schwastek's talking about how Wantje had stocked the ponds at number ten with some three- and four-footers, not quite fully grown, supposedly able to survive in the chillier water for a week or two. Hell, I thought, Wantje's gotta be putting that bullshit out there to scare me. Because there are no alligators or crocodiles in Michigan except in zoos and aquariums and maybe a bathtub here or there. Although I do remember reading about some fool who tossed a baby gator into the AuSable and it wound up growing big enough to make some poor family's dachshund into dinner. That sounded a little iffy too, but I read it in an Internet newspaper—or maybe Reddit?—so I can't totally discount it. The more I think about it, the more I think, shit, gators are sissies next to snappers anyway. Snappers don't have to be hungry to bite your left nut off. They do it just for fun.

Still. Gators? Really, Wantje?

Now it's true I haven't been to Splendid Acres in a week or two, but not because I'm afraid or paranoid or Wantje got to me or anything like that. This very night, beneath a full moon, I'm sliding on my butt through the shoreline mud of the pond that lies further from the tenth tee. The one with the pipe. I pause to survey the scene as my flippers disappear into the black water. Things look normal enough. I slip deeper into the water, up to my belly, feeling the heels of my flippers push into the slime. In the cattails across the pond, maybe forty feet away, moonlight glints off a dark ridge of nubs protruding from the surface of the water. Bullshit, I think. It's gotta be a log. Or a shadow. Or maybe Wantje planted one of those half-assed plastic gators dumb people use to try to frighten ducks and geese. I'm not falling for it any more than the birds do. I pull my mask down, bite down on my snorkel, and flick on my headlamp. I'm going under. It's treasure time.

I can usually hold my breath for a little more than a minute, but tonight, for some reason, I come up short and have to abort my first dive after about forty seconds. Still, I stuff a respectable nine or ten balls into my bag. When I re-emerge for a breath, I tread water for a few seconds to look around. Whatever I saw across the pond before is gone. I tell myself I probably imagined it in the first place. No worries, all is well. I dive back down, headed for the pipe. Halfway down I stop for a second, take another look around. Not much visible in the murk. I can just barely see the pipe below. Something seems to have kicked up the bottom silt. I go back up for a quick breath, decide I'll make one healthy plunge to the pipe, snag a couple of dozen balls and call it a night, come back tomorrow.

The pipe, though, looks weirdly naked as I dip near it. Almost as if someone else, some other diver—no, not Wantje, no way—got here before me. Or maybe the balls just sank into the sediment beneath. I grab the pipe with one hand and pull myself close, wedging one of my flippers beneath a flange so I won't bob up. With my other hand I root around in the mire, trying to scare up some balls. Just like that, a flurry of them, white and yellow and orange, pop out of the muck.

Jackpot.

I snatch at them with one hand, stuffing them two-by-two into my sack, while my other hand steadies me and the flipper under the pipe holds me in place. My chest tightens with the urge for fresh air but it's only a few kicks to the surface and I'll be fine.

One last ball, a Titleist Pro VI, its dimples glistening in the lamp light, is within reach. I lunge and—got it. But as I pitch forward, my flipper twists and something snaps in my knee. The pain tears through it like a steak knife, like something chomped the back of the knee, shredding my hamstring.

Don't scream, I tell myself. Don't panic. Don't take a breath. I can't free my leg because it hurts too much when I pull. My lungs are on fire. I give in. I exhale. Pond water gushes into my mouth and throat, the taste of a ditch filled with drowned raccoons. My stomach turns over. I want to puke. I rip off my mask and look up. The moon is a hazy blur on the surface of the water. Something pushes through it, distorting the fuzzy glow. Is that a hand? A hand reaching down to save me? I stretch my arm upward, but the hand is out of reach. A wave of yellow light washes over me. Then it's white. Then black.

You got me, Wantje. You got me good.

Kathleen McGookey
WITHOUT INSTRUCTIONS

I can't leave the sky alone—I keep ransacking its pale silence for a sign. One word and your voice is full of feathers or chalk, *fine* or *please*. What are you waiting for in your little box, all elbows and knees, dawn washing over you? We might as well talk about anything else. Dawn's as good a word as any, reassuring as breath. A tiny radio plays inside your silence; a faraway telephone rings. I fold news from home to reach you later, fear lingering like a return address.

Melinda Wolf
ACT AS IF

The squadron is coming for you.
Contrails fade into the darkening sky—
letters, messages, white rags of surrender
beneath the bemused countenance
of the moon with its own golden prompts.
You type "help" into the waiting mouth of your
computer then "act as if":
>   I am not running out of time.
>   I have a million chances to find just
>   What it is I'm looking for.
>   I decipher the countermeasures
>   Of angels.
>   It is all countermeasures.
>   There are angels.
As if this interface, you, the sky,
presented an algorithm, something other
than subterfuge, the heft of apocalyptic curiosity,
this endless search
with no good results.

Catherine Anderson
THE WORD *ACHE*, WITH ITS OWN SADNESS

Once a rhyme with the word *match*
in Middle English, that soft
ch at the end again,
hovering like a touch.
Through the ages of English,
the word also meant a longing after loss,
the remainder of pain.
In the plural, if you can imagine
multiple losses — a home,
a country, a family — you hear
a word that comes close
to the sound of *ashes*,
yet the *e* always silent
because aches are imperceptible
to the one sitting beside the other
who yearns in daylight,
who hesitates to speak
among strangers.

Melinda Wolf
THE LANGUAGE OF HORSESHOES

Our words are heavy
      horseshoes, iron rainbows,
            archways into dark tunnels —
                  these once spitting hot
                        iron rods brandished
                              into benevolence,
                      bent beyond recognition —
                poor birds, the sand forgives
            their heavy thuds,
        the clang that much louder
in its solid silence.

Caitlin Johnson
THE PROUST EFFECT

How does this coffee smell
like the apartment where our
mother moved beyond herself
in the slanted afternoon sun
and the promise of the pool
and its clear-blue ability to
press magic into my small body,
render me mermaid, render me
untouched by this choice, hope
still threaded into each of my
little ribs? That summer, this
coffee, and in between a grief
so big it has its own heartbeat.

Kaylee Schofield
SONG FOR THE END OF THE WORLD

There is nothing for grief but grief.
Say the word, rote magic, until it goes,
moon rising silent over the pines.
Bear witness to your self,
this pool of blooded gravel and snow.
It will not go away, no matter how much you
want. A mouth
that burrows into itself
like the nautilus, a pale balloon
hovering just out of reach.

Grip the string. Light a fire, a small one,
and burn all the letters you wrote,
but at the last minute, change your mind.
There is a drawer for such things. Keep them
there until you are ready to forget them
with the birthday cards and the pay stubs
you saved up for a drought that never came.
Above all, hold your own heart
like the broken beetle that escaped
through a door at the last possible moment.

Your name is what it was, a crystal jar.
Your name: sound wave on sound wave,
city at night backlit by painted metal,
stagehands turning the crank
on a distant sea.

Onna Solomon
TALL TALE

I looked for the path
and found it, wound my way

through the woods, haunted by
stories I needed to hear.

I entered the house
and bowed at her feet. She blessed me

with a prick of her needle
on my breast. No one is lost

forever. The trail always leads us
home, beyond the terrifying

beasts tamed, in the end, by love.
You must believe me. I emerged

unscathed, mended
with a golden thread.

Hannah Rowell
WAKE

This house was a restful golem
with wood bones and brick skin.
Two eyes listless, yellow glass,
squinting down at tree faces.
Air rattled vents when it yawned
and stuck in its skull, we listened
to the clocks.
They pulsed, like
drumming blood
in the halls.

Up these stairs, like
the notches of a spine, there
was quiet that locked
between us. The click of a key
unheard

in my own dark room —
in the attic, looking anywhere
but right down the hall.
We were trapped
inside the skull.

In the yellow window,
one might have seen our silhouettes,
pupils to each eye.
Outside, the snow settled
with no silverbells to see.

There are kinds of steady
that only exist in memory,
imprinted as a whisper on the door
until the sound of absence rises,
opens our eyes
and wakes the house.

Kimberly Gibson-Tran
NIGHT THINGS

The air is a calamity of prayer. When one pitch submits, another rises, matches it, a roiling, threaded storm. I can hear the group's fervent murmuring, home playing sick in the cozy dark of my parents' room one house over. Cold and tense, the water bed buoys me into an utter alone. I flee the room, the house, leave the porchlight on in my rush, the slap of screen door. Wind dense with mist, I zoom my bike around the compound, past our house, last in the rowhouses—the middle unit lit with the life of the prayer meeting, ours lit with the light I'd left on. Past the orchard, tennis court, the nurse-aids' dorms, the clinic, water tower, gatehouse, flame tree, wall. Everything hummed. From all edges. I could not break the encumbering dark. Not the low-hanging orchard limes nor the north-leaning teak trees down to the watery fields, nor the road lying flat and black to the south. I stop at the east end, look out to the invisible mountains, feel their thereness. No singing. The meeting's breaking up. In another push I am home and only beginning to see my mistake. Our living room floor, carpet, couch, table, hutch—writhing, a sea of squirming bodies in black mass. Outside, the finest films of paper, a stirred whirlwind of disembodied wings. I had summoned the beings with the light, and the screen clipped them. The fan spread the horde to all corners, a hundred hundred thousand twisted things I, wretched, swept away.

Ellen Lord
FAMILY HEIRLOOM
—for Guss Lord (10/28/49 – 02/19/23)

My brother Guss called to ask about Dad's trombone. His eight-year-old grandson wants to play it. Who knows why, except that he's a smart kid, wired tight, and likes a lot of drama. We got drama. That horn is bigger than he is. Guss wants me to call our sister. She was the last one to have custody of the trombone. He wouldn't think to call her himself because that is what he does—comes up with ideas and dictates directions. I smile. I listen.

I know what he really wants…to talk to his big sister. He knows I'm worried. He's been diagnosed with cirrhosis. Not good. Home from the hospital for a week—again. The details are predictable: Vietnam veteran. PTSD and Agent Orange dreams—a fine recipe for mayhem. Just add an Irish-Catholic upbringing for spice. He's a Jackpine Savage, born and raised in the U.P. Comes from our family of bootleggers, hunters, and yellow dog Democrats. Most of the men have a cache of guns, tribal loyalty, and a penchant for mischief. They cleave to civilized women who love them, of course.

Anyway, yes, I'm worried. I know that he knows that I know he's drinking. He stops for a few months at a time but now, I can tell by the slur in his voice—he's back at it. We dance around the topic and talk about the trombone. It must be a hundred years old. Dad played in high school and then passed it on to me in 1962. I gave it to our sister for her kid and on it goes—one of the few family heirlooms. I tell him I'll check with the tribe and get back to him. Then…there is silence on the line.

He's not ready to say goodbye and neither am I.

He tells me this story: He went to the bar early yesterday. He's a day crowd regular—got his favorite stool. The joint opens at 11 a.m. and he likes to leave by 3 p.m. before cops are out and deer aren't apt to be bounding across the road. As he drives into the parking lot, he runs over a glass beer bottle. BAM…blows a tire. Damn! There's no one around so he calls AAA for road service. Amazingly, two guys show up in less than twenty minutes. NED'S TIRE is stenciled on a rusted pickup truck. Ned slogs out of his truck. He's a big guy, grey-bearded to his waist, reminiscent of *Duck Dynasty*.

—Which tire is it?
—Da one dat's flat.

—Got any tools?...a jack?

—Fuck ya... yur da tire guy. Doncha have yur own tools?

—I was in a rush to hep ya and forgot my tools in da other truck.

—Ya, mutherfucker, I got tools.

Guss gets out and cracks a beer. Gives one to Ned. Ned cracks a beer then bends over to inspect the tire and exposes his butt crack. The other skinny, toothless guy gets out, cracks a beer and finds Guss's tools. The fix takes all afternoon. They break for lunch in the bar. They git'er done.

Guss laughs — *Ya, you can't make this shit up. That's how we do it in the U.P.*

I laugh. Everything is all right, even when it isn't.

John Randall
ONE ROAD

Mark of leaving, memory contusion discolored by time.
Experimental car door mutters yesterday's weather. The wide
thumb of a Saturday afternoon eclipsed by eventide even when
sobriquet sojourns unspool from undropped acorns. Where will I go
to tire myself, to sweat myself pounds lighter? Borne of sunscreen
under floppy hat, searching the breeze for mint. I don't want to
unwire myself but every hair on my body is magnified. That's when
the phlebotomist leveled with me and said, "I don't know if I should
tell you this, but most of the good writers don't become famous until
they're dead." Among the dust and the dry fields, surrounded again
by engines. That was twenty years ago. I am in the blue hollows,
I am in the cold van. Makeshift huts and lean-tos, living on the
sidewalk. There is only one road in and one road out, one road.
Moonlight wades into spent grass.

Kimberly Gibson-Tran
FOXES OF WAT PHO

after Ted Hughes

The bats sound
the humid air
with their screeling.
All day they hang

sleeping and preening
peeling and unpeeling
themselves like bananas
in need of a breeze.

Whenever we visit
the bat temple
my dad has to repeat
the story of his student,

years ago, who took
urine to the eye.
The moral: be careful
who you look up to.

The sound really is
a wonder, and anywhere
there's wonder
there's a need

to worship. This
temple is well-placed.
The monks have extra
sweeping. They do it

barefoot, ignoring
the gossip and kisses
in the canopy.
A bat gets electrified

now and then, clings
sharp hot stink
to the telephone line,
a burnt banana bloom.

Into purple dusk
the black mass looms,
shadows the city,
falls over lowlands,

the river bridge,
feasting, we think,
in the orchard
just out of town,

an offering. They gnaw,
fox-faced, fox-teethed,
on the soft meats
of mangos, tangerines,

piss them sweetly
back into the ground.
They resoil the soil.

They reenter the dark
echo-hole of the head.

Paula Fernandez
AMERICAN PASTORAL

Everyone has a home—for better or worse—a place they feel they belong. Ours had seen better days was really only half a house since the roof caved in over the back bedroom. There were no locks on our home. Just a sullen one-eyed dog in the yard and a double-barrel by the door.

life in the country

In winter, thick sheets of ice glinted like stained glass on the insides of the windows. Bull snakes shrugged up the hot water pipes and curled together under the sinks. We called them our pipe cozies and left them in peace dreaming of spring. When we turned on the lights, our shy, skittering landlords—shiny, winged, shimmering in onyx and amber—tucked themselves discretely away into the walls, behind the cabinets, under the sugar bowl.

must have been

Every day we bathed in the haze of swirling smoke puffed out in long sinuous ribbons from the large, sad man in boxers enthroned on the couch. All were anointed in that gauzy yellow glaze—the walls, the self-pitying houseplant, our hair, our clothes—so that when we left our home to go to school or church, that pungent perfume preceded us, and everywhere we went smelled just like home.

so beautiful

Mary Jo Firth Gillett
FEAR

I must have been six when Mr. Morgan, my best friend's
father, killed the garter snake in their backyard, chopping off

its head with the edge of a shovel. I tried to look away
but the headless body writhed back and forth.

A bead of blood rose from the point of decapitation as if
it were a bullet point trying to shout something important.

Mr. Morgan stood there, proud and manly, having protected
his family from the serpent, a harmless, helpful creature

with beautiful, cool skin, skin my mother, the gardener,
called *jewel-like*. I stared hard at a man I'd never known

to be cruel, watched him jump away from the snake in a fever,
as if it would attack. Today on the news, more bombs,

rubble, refugees, and a line of infants laid in a row,
wrapped round and round in white—little cocoons of never.

Chris Cochran
RESURFACING

Wolfie sits in a foot of hose water, surrounded by fish with magnets for mouth I hook one with his toy pole and reel it in, pretending it puts up a fight.

"Get in," he says. I dip my toes into the freezing water and shudder.

"Your dad doesn't exactly fit in a kiddie pool." He meows. When h hears his parents laugh, his meowing turns into a chorus.

"Three more minutes," Rae tells him. She eases herself out of the hammock and heads inside to start dinner. When I return my attention to Wolfie, he's pointing a tiny red water pistol at me, like a little gangster. He squeezes the trigger, but nothing comes out, and I laugh as he tosses the empty gun aside in frustration.

"I'm bored. Let's just go in," he says. As he stands, I step toward th pool to help but slip on the wet grass. The plastic edge of the pool buckles under the weight of my knee. Wolfie falls hard on his backside. He's fine, but I'm flustered in that moment of uncertainty when he looks to me for reassurance.

Rae comes back outside when she hears his cries. "Daddy accidentally did the wrong thing!" he says, as she scoops him up in her arms. His chin resting on her shoulder, he shoots me a look as cold as the pool water.

I'm sure Wolfie forgot what happened within the hour, yet I'm still reflecting on it weeks later. What is most unsettling is the familiarity of the incident. I can't shake the feeling that the toy pistol, the icy water, the cold look—it all points to something within my subconscious, a memory trying to find its way to the surface.

Wolfie pushes against the straps as I unbuckle his car seat. A ball of uncontainable energy, he's writhing out of my arms as I attempt to wrangle him from the backseat. Once his feet hit the ground, he yells "Grandma!" and runs toward my mom, who matches his excitement with her own. Rae and I exchange smiles, relieved to be on the precipice of a fe hours to ourselves.

We visit for a while on my parents' deck that overlooks the lake, glistening in the late summer sun. Rafts anchored a short distance from th eastern shoreline are teeming with kids, their shrieks of laughter echoing across the lake's surface. They play with frantic intensity, understanding that autumn is near with winter on its heels; meanwhile, Wolfie plays a farming simulator on his grandma's phone.

"So, where are you two headed?" my dad asks. We plan to go to a nature reserve, hike the trails carved out by those before us.

"You should go to the open house," my mom says, providing no further explanation. Rae looks to me for help, but I don't have a clue.

"Better hurry, ends in about an hour," my dad says.

Rae asks, "Open house?"

"Our old house is for sale," my mom says.

Wolfie looks up from the phone. "You're selling your house?"

"No, our old house. The house your dad grew up in."

"Oh." An advertisement for an online casino flashes on the screen. He closes it and continues collecting eggs from his chickens.

"Is there something else Wolfie can play with?" I ask.

"Oh no, he's fine," my mom responds.

"They've done a bunch of renovations," my dad explains.

"Wolfie, give that back to your grandma." He ignores me. Rae takes over after noticing my frustration and calmly coaxes him into handing over the phone.

A pontoon passes across the lake. I imagine fish with magnetic mouths bobbing atop the waves left in its wake.

✸✸✸

I have had dreams in which I'll notice something is slightly askew, like the curtains are a different color or the hands of a clock are spinning in the wrong direction, and this realization will bring me back to consciousness. Standing inside my early childhood home, my eyes trace the circumference of a round floor medallion embedded within the foyer tile, not unlike what one would expect to find in a hotel lobby. It's one of those touch-ups that artificially adds value to a house before selling, and its incongruence is disorienting. I wonder if this will be the moment my eyes finally open and that none of this will have happened, that I'll wake up in my room, just a kid, and come down the steps and grandpa will be here—and it will all have been a dream.

Rae already teased me for ringing the doorbell, and now she delivers another lesson in open house etiquette as I take off my shoes. I suppose old habits die hard. The realtor is chatting with another couple in the kitchen. We sneak upstairs. I show Rae which bedroom was mine, and we marvel at its spaciousness. It's difficult not to compare it to Wolfie's small room. Forty years ago, my parents purchased this house for a fraction of its current listing price on one salary, yet Rae and I could only dream of affording the down payment.

The realtor doesn't even acknowledge us as we head into the basement. It is clear she knows we are not serious buyers, which is fine. I'd rather not pretend, anyway.

I walk down the steps and it's Christmas morning. A giant red bow adorns a new bicycle, but I am looking down at the baseball cards I found in my stocking and walk right past it without noticing. My parents laugh, so I look up to see what all the fuss is about.

"Did you hear me?"

I blink. The shag carpet is gone, replaced with hardwood flooring. The floral wallpaper steamed off, replaced by neutral gray paint.

"Hmm?"

"Wow. I lost you there for a moment," Rae says.

"Sorry. It's just…memories."

"Is this where you lost your virginity?" she asks, already laughing.

"You know we moved when I was ten, right?"

"That's why it's funny."

I sit down on a firm couch, expecting to sink into sagging cushions. In front of me, an old tube television nestles inside an outdated entertainment center that looks remarkably like the one I had growing up. "I can remember having a bunch of friends over for a birthday party. We stayed up all night in this basement playing video games."

Rae sits down beside me. "Why would they not replace this?" she asks, and upon reexamination, I realize something improbable. This does not just look like the entertainment center we had growing up; it's the same one. This is where I kept my Sega Genesis and VHS tapes, and this television — this is the one I watched as a child.

The memory that began its ascent weeks ago emerges. This is where I sat and watched a son murder his father.

❄ ❄ ❄

"Where were your parents?" Rae asks. I purse my lips and shake my head, sending beads of sweat cascading down my brow. We are at the end of a three-mile loop trail we used to hike before Wolfie was born. Despite the trail being relatively flat, my legs ache. They never used to, and I grow skeptical that anything gets easier with age.

I had told Rae what I remembered: about the son and his father ice fishing; about the son throwing hot coffee in his father's face, pushing him into the rectangular hole that was carved out of the ice; about the father's face beneath the ice and how he desperately tried to resurface but could not locate the fishing hole; about how white his teeth were when he finally succumbed and took his last gasp, allowing the icy water to fill his lungs.

We make it back to the parking lot. Rae waits outside the passenger side while I try to determine which pocket of the backpack she stuffed the keys into. She is typing and scrolling on her phone, which finally has reception now that we are out of the woods. "Could it have been one of those made-for-TV movies?" she asks.

"Yeah, maybe." I doubt she will have any more luck finding it than I am having finding the keys. "Which pocket?"

"It's the small one," Rae says, which does not help. She walks over and unzips a pocket I didn't realize existed, fishes out the keys, and hands them over. "Look what else I found." She holds up her screen, revealing a video titled *The Stranger Within.*

I grab her phone and scrub the video ahead, previewing the thumbnail images. Near the halfway mark, I see two men in winter gear standing on top of a frozen lake. "How did you…?"

Rae explains her search terms, but it's white noise; I have become singularly focused on the release date—1990. I was five, the same age as Wolfie. I point this out to Rae.

We drive in silence for a while. I can tell she wants to ask but is giving me room to suggest it first. Maybe it is necessary that I revisit my childhood trauma to confront it head-on. I don't actually believe this, but my morbid curiosity wins out.

"Movie night?" I say.

***

We tried to keep Wolfie awake, but the late afternoon car ride lulled him to sleep. When we got home, I carried him inside like a baby, supporting his neck while his loose limbs dangled. He didn't stir as I gently placed him on our couch.

"Do we wake him up?" Rae asks.

"If we don't, he's never going to sleep tonight." Wolfie snores loudly and shifts into a more comfortable position.

"But he's so cute," Rae says.

I rub his back to wake him and witness the look of glassy-eyed confusion on his face as he surveys his surroundings. "We're home, buddy. Time to get up."

We get him to eat a small dinner, read a few books, and eventually have him tucked in for the night, not too long after his normal bedtime. It takes longer than usual for him to fall asleep. When we notice his breathing has steadied, Rae starts the popcorn, and I cast the movie from my laptop to the living room television.

The video is so grainy that I have to squint, trying to give definition to the pixelated shadows on the screen, to reconcile this version with what I remember watching as a child. In the opening scene, a boy named Mark is abducted from a grocery store while his single mother, Mare, is distracted by the owner's sales pitch for a breakfast cereal that is clearly Cap'n Crunch, unnamed for copyright reasons.

Sixteen years later, someone claiming to be Mark returns. He seems sketchy from the start, but Mare so badly wants to believe that he is her son that she quickly sheds her skepticism. Dan, her boyfriend, is highly suspicious, however, and it's him, not the boy's actual father (who had died before the movie began), whose tortured face would appear trapped beneath the ice.

We laugh at some of the film's cheesier moments, but it's not a bad psychological thriller, especially for a film without a theatrical release. I am surprisingly on edge. When Mark and Dan make their way onto the frozen lake, my heart beats faster, my muscles tighten.

After a heated exchange between the two men in which Dan threatens to contact the police, Mark awkwardly delivers a seemingly sincere speech. Dan lets his guard down, only to have coffee thrown in his face before Mark shoves him into the fishing hole.

For as much as I had confused the plot, the action in this scene plays out almost exactly as I remember. The camera alternates between a low-angle shot beneath the ice that captures Dan's attempt to surface and a high-angle shot above the ice that reveals Mark forcing him back underwater. Eventually, Mark's fist connects and sends Dan drifting under the ice.

Rae squeezes my hand. I shift uncomfortably on the couch.

Mark yells for his "mom," screams that Dan "fell in" and that he can't reach him. Mare dangerously runs across the ice while Mark pretends to be in distress. She can't find Dan until, with a bit of movie magic, he punches his arm through the ice. Mare desperately wipes the snow from the surface and reveals Dan's panicked face below. She hacks at the ice but it's no use; he's inches away, but there is nothing she can do. Mare holds his hand and weeps as his lungs give out. His face becomes a fixture beneath the ice, where it has been buried within my subconscious for the past three decades.

A small voice behind me says, "Dad?" and I turn around to see Wolfie standing behind the couch, frozen in fear.

❖ ❖ ❖

On Sunday mornings, Rae and I like to make fancy coffee and pretend we are at a cafe as we sit across from each other at the high top tucked in our kitchen corner. We are comfortable sitting quietly, enjoying each other's company. This morning, however, the silence is noticeable.

We didn't finish the movie last night. Rae walked Wolfie back to his room while I stayed on the couch in disbelief at our carelessness. I tried to convince myself that he didn't actually see it, but I couldn't deny the look of horror on his face. We needed to sit down and talk with him this morning, but how does one provide context for cold-blooded murder to a five-year-old?

A knock at the door breaks the silence. My dad lets himself in and places a bag of bagels on the table as he takes a seat. Rae gets up, grabs a mug from the cupboard, and pours him a cup of coffee.

"Wolfgang still sleeping?"

"Yeah. He was up late last night." I stare into the dregs of my coffee.

Rae places my dad's mug on the table, and he takes a sip. "How was the open house?"

We talk about all the renovations, about how outrageous home prices have become. I tell him about the hideous floor medallion in the foyer.

"Your mom always hated that thing."

"Wait, really? I thought that was new."

"No, it was there when we bought the house. Your mom insisted we cover it up with that colorful rag rug, the one that's in our basement now."

"Huh." I spread cream cheese on a bagel. "I do not remember that at all."

Wolfie's bedroom door opens, and he bolts across the hallway to the bathroom. I lock eyes with Rae, a nonverbal acknowledgement that we're no more prepared to talk with him now than we were last night.

"What we remember, what we forget—it's all so arbitrary," my dad says.

"Sometimes," I concede. "Not always."

"Well, I hope you're right," Rae tells my dad. "We messed up with Wolfie last night. I'd be okay if he soon forgot about it." She gives him an abbreviated version of our movie night.

"I wouldn't waste time beating yourselves up over it. Lord knows we made mistakes with this one," he says, nodding his head toward me, "but he ended up alright."

"That's debatable," Rae says.

"Just make sure Wolfgang knows he is loved. That's all that matters."

Wolfie walks into the kitchen and lights up when he sees his grandpa. As they greet each other with a hug, Rae leads me into the living room.

"I think we should—"

"I'll talk to him this time," I say.

After my dad leaves, Wolfie and I head to the basement. I am not sure where to begin. It's him that breaks the ice with an apology; he says he is sorry for sneaking out of his room, and I am devastated that he thinks he is in trouble. So I pull myself up out of the frozen lake and start by telling Wolfie that I love him.

Catherine Anderson
STOLEN

In my life, I've taken it all—the meat,
the skin, the root, the water, the petroleum
that fuels my going, steals
the air from someone else.

I've taken the feathers, the magnetic
bones, the gold,
the healing mint, the willow bark.

I would have stolen refracted sunlight
in the wing of an indigo bunting
to sketch a picture, if I could.

I cannot think of a word for this,
yet there must be one.

Without even knowing, I stole a bit of cobalt—
the demon element
powering the lithium-ion battery
of cell phones, mined by children working
in the open pits of the Democratic Republic of Congo.
Cobalt in its other form shines
with the blue pigment of its name.
In an art store, I found a thin, sharp
pencil in this color for the shade
it casts in shadow.
I thought that was all cobalt was, a color.
I bought it to enhance the blue
throat of my bird.
There is no word, no equivalent—
to draw a bird, to steal from a child.

Julia Lewis
ON ROLEPLAYING

The Dungeon Master

I am sitting behind the Dungeon Master's screen, a ruby dragon curling around the outward-facing panels. The tension is palpable as I rattle the dice in my hand, eyeing each of my players to garner their reactions. No one is speaking—a rarity during these events—but there is the shuffling of papers, Aaron's heavy breathing, the clink of Rachel's beer bottle as she sets it on the tabletop. I count down in my head, putting on a show of building the tension, until finally I release the dice. They roll across the table, making sharp sounds that disrupt the tense silence, until they eventually come to a stop at the base of my screen.
Five, 13, 9, and 20.

Lewis sucks in a short, delighted gasp as he sneaks a glance behind the screen. A natural 20, for those unaccustomed to the rules of Dungeons & Dragons, is a critical hit, in this case meaning that the dragon I am commanding critically struck the party of players, almost certainly decimating their characters.

From the bark of laughter that erupts from Lewis, the rest of the players understand what has happened and visibly deflate. Rachel takes another swig of her beer, Aaron frowns at his character's miniature figurine on the playmat as if willing it to run off the table to safety, and Leah flips her pencil around, ready to erase and replace her life value. Lewis continues laughing.

I look across the battlefield, at the miniatures engaged in the battle for the hoard of a lifetime—the dragon's treasure room—and I know what I have to do. I am the Dungeon Master, and it is my responsibility to give the players a good time, to make sure they have fun as they take on the dark creatures of the realm. They play the adventurers, the heroes. My role is that of the navigator, of the narrator, of the world they adventure through. I take this role very seriously—I've been on the other side of that Dungeon Master's screen, felt the excitement of victory and the rage of defeat—and above all else want my players to enjoy the game.

I take a breath, slow and deliberate, and prepare to speak.

A Textbook Definition

The French-based word "role" refers to the function assumed by a person or thing in a particular situation. For instance, my cat's role in my life is as a wise sage who never questions my decisions and instead gives me love and the occasional tongue-bath cleaning. My role in my cat's life is that of the almighty food-giver and poop-cleaner. I see myself as her caregiver; maybe she sees me more as a maid.

The Old English word "play" refers to engaging in an activity for enjoyment and recreation rather than a serious or practical purpose. It can also mean to take part in a sport, represent a character in a theatrical performance, perform on a musical instrument, move lightly or quickly so as to appear and disappear, or to allow a fish to exhaust itself pulling against a line before reeling it in. That last one surprised me too. It's almost cruel, how such a fun, enjoyable word could mean something related to death.

Put these two words together and you get "roleplay" which refers to the acting out of a particular person or character or to participate in a role-playing game.

"A harlot? Yes, but a traitor, never!"

I share a birthday (August 7th) with Margaretha Beertruida MacLeod, better known by her stage name Mata Hari. Margaretha began her life as the daughter of a hat shop owner, married a Dutch Colonial Army Captain who beat her senselessly, divorced him and moved to Paris after their son died of syphilis, tried her hand as a circus horse rider, became famous for her exotic dancing, took on the role of successful courtesan, fell in love with a Russian pilot during World War I, and then became a French spy because the French told her she would only be allowed to see her beloved, wounded pilot if she spied on the Germans for them.

On October 15th, 1917, Margaretha was executed by firing squad for giving names of French spies to the Germans. Before the shots took her life, Margaretha defiantly blew a kiss to the firing squad. She took on many roles in her life, but this final one is my favorite to think about—a woman who took her life and her sexuality into her own hands, even in her last moments.

In the Bedroom

"Sexual role play is a pleasurable and erotic means of validating parts of ourselves which we may have previously dismissed, ignored, split off from, or even shunned."

—Miya Yamanouchi, *Embrace Your Sexual Self: A Practical Guide for Women*

"Millions more adults regularly indulge in bondage, spanking, role-play, and so on as foreplay. For them, these are erotic games that add spice to monogamous relationships, extend the arousal period, and enhance orgasm."
—Gloria Brame, *Come Hither: A Commonsense Guide to Kinky Sex*

"Damn right we roleplay."
—My mother, sitting around having a nice cup of coffee

Psychologically Charged

In psychology, "roleplay" is used in reference to the way a person unconsciously acts out or performs a particular role in accordance with the perceived expectations of society. My mother, now celebrating her fifteenth anniversary with her wife, spent the first thirty years of her life pretending to be straight because she thought it was what you were supposed to do. She once told me that she punched a guy in the face when she was sixteen because he called her a "dyke"—not because she considered the word a slur, but because she was desperate to avoid being labeled homosexual.

As the oldest of four daughters in my family, I am the black sheep as the only one who dates men. The societal expectations of my childhood home are much different than what my mother faced. I wonder at the freedom that has allowed my siblings and me to explore.

The Actor

Growing up, I loved theater and spent most of my high school career staying after school, involving myself in some capacity in the theater arts department. I acted in the fall play, directed and choreographed the spring musical, and occasionally did sound and lighting for the band performances. My favorite job was standing onstage and playing pretend as another person. Positioned there, the lights burning through me, the silhouettes of the audience shuffling in their seats—I was exhilarated. I loved every moment from my first entrance stage left to my final bow.

I loved acting enough that I considered going into it as a profession. I had friends from the school and the local civic theater that were dead set on pursuing theatre careers. Two of them moved to New York with the dream of Broadway fame, one headed to a prestigious college to study opera, and another made his way to California in the hopes of moving up in the world of film. I wanted to follow in their footsteps right up until I spoke with my family about it.

"It's a wonderful hobby," my mother called it, "but not a career."

"You'd be great at it," added my stepmother, "but I don't think it would pay the bills."

"Are you even good enough?" my grandmother asked.

Being an actor was never a real option for me, I guess. It was just one of those roles we long to play as we lie awake at night, thoughts of what could have been dancing through our brains.

Bogus Beggar

From 2009 to 2013, Gary Thompson made as much as $100,000 annually by panhandling in Lexington, Kentucky. This amount was due, in most part, to his severe disabilities that inspired people to support him monetarily.

In February 2013, Gary Thompson was arrested and charged with two counts of theft by deception for faking those disabilities in order to trick passersby into giving him more money. This "bogus beggar," as he became known, would pretend to be mentally and/or physically disabled by slowing his speech and stuttering and, on certain occasions, unnecessarily utilizing a wheelchair.

Some have called him an entrepreneur, the next Jordan Belfort. I call him an asshole.

The Protector

At one point my stepfather beat my mother so badly that we could hear her crying on the second floor from my room in the basement. My two younger sisters, Jasmine and Josephine, were five and three at the time, and we huddled in my closet with a flashlight and a book. I read to them that night, as loudly as I could, in hopes that I would drown out the scene above us. They curled in at my sides, their little hands gripping my sweatshirt like a lifeline, and I smelled the sweat dripping off them as the temperature rose to uncomfortable degrees in the small room. I wouldn't have let them leave, though, even if they had wanted to.

In that little closet, my clothes pushed aside to make room for the terrified trio, I found my place as protector, even just momentarily. It was a role I didn't play as much as I should have during my time sharing a home with my sisters, but it's one that I'm most proud of taking on.

I wish it hadn't been as necessary a role as it was.

Egyptian Dollhouses

The earliest known examples of dollhouses were found in the Egyptian tombs and were created nearly five thousand years ago. They were wooden and depicted servants, furnishings, boats, livestock, pets, and other staples of Egyptian culture. Even then, people knew that there were roles that needed to be practiced before someone could accurately step into the position.

The Mainstays

I play many roles in my life: sister, daughter, game master, friend, wife, cat mom, educator, writer, artist, nerd, employee, supervisor, and so many more. Every moment pulls me from one role to the next, every conversation and every turn. To some I am one thing and to their neighbor something completely different. There are roles I want to play, roles I cherish, and then there are roles I would rather give up forever. I have chosen some and others have been forced upon me.

But for now, I do what I can and play the part set before me. My players need to know what becomes of them, of their steadfast adventurers caught between fortune and dragon fire. I open my mouth to speak, to illustrate with words what has just transpired, and the party goes quiet again, waiting in anticipation as I take the role of the mighty dragon.

John Walser
I LISTEN FOR YOU
for Julie

1.
The asphalt dries to chalk
before the next storms:
September afternoon downpours
intense scattered.

Upstairs the radio plays
but I don't mind it:
not for now:

the DJ's voice like the rain
the treble and bass
more pronounced
than any words
nothing that gets in my way
of listening and wanting:

even the commercials are just
electricity sparking.

2.
Between downpours:
the sky, a gradation:

silver east:
the matted floss cotton wood above:
that sky like drizzle itself:

but to the west: what builds what fills in:
I say: *Density.* I say: *Deluge*
I say: *To come* as the rain starts
a constant patter and shifts to heavy.

The next staggering pushes new tar
darkened asphalt glare.

I want to be walking
with you somewhere
when this kind of storm hits:
when most couples
find doorways or restaurants
or taxis to wait out to soak.

I want to know where we are
by the sighting of a spire
the tolling of church bells
the shuffle of city squares
by landmarks
we recognize from earlier in the morning
by the cathedral lost behind buildings
and trees and wrong turns
and not caring.

I want to stand with you
on a plaza where pigeons and dust
a different sunshine, a different sky
fly like an oil paint banner
pulled taut over our newness.

I want a drenching:
hair, shoes, glasses:
every inch of us:
so we have to strip
as best we can
before we get in the car
to drive to whatever hotel
we are staying at
whatever store where
we buy cheap tennis shoes
and strange socks.

3.
Let the room have a shifting view:
trees and clouds we've never known
walking paths that lead to mud meadows
the crack of autumn weeds.

4.
We can rent it for a couple nights
a week or two: a month:
or as long as we want to stay.

We will find the smaller pleasures:
to send our laundry out each Thursday:
to have only two forks
two spoons, two bowls
two plates, two knives:

or only one knife we pass between us
as we chop cheese and vegetables.
We will buy secondhand bicycles
and ride them into the country:
eggs at a farm stand
someone who makes barrel wine
the bottles roughly corked.

We will follow only our stomachs:
the butchery of rabbits
roasters, lambs

because happiness is moving
toward, toward, toward with you.

5.
Upstairs: the radio off now.
I listen for you
but you are quiet now
silent as –

6.
And on a Friday
(although days won't matter to us, will they?)
when the rain comes
subtle steady as the grey sky, as plastic

I want us
to be standing on stones
watching a fishing boat
(you name the colors)
tantalus leaning:
a lowtide harbor
of nets and shallows
of kelp, of shellfish
mussels, clams the size
of teaplates
that breathe bubbles
into the mud sand
into the pressed surface

the hull boards dry creaking
deeper than that thunder
that works like rubber
somewhere beyond

the glow of the high grey sky
of here and now.

Joanne Esser
WHAT YOU NEED

A steady silver rain pours out
over the gray world on an ordinary
morning. Drenching for hours
the field, wildflowers, soil
and all the birds off somewhere dry
in hidden nests, keeping quiet.

And you, too: keep quiet for a few hours,
let your thoughts fizz like that silver sheen,
shushshushshushshush, ceaseless sheet
of velvet, of plenty. Enough to hear, to drink,
to soak in, though you hadn't known
how dry you were.

Esther Walker
AFTER THE STORM: PANCAKES, TOGETHER

We needed food. The interstate had shut down. The travel peanut butter jar my mother carried had been scraped clean hours before. The cookies and chips my father kept in the trunk were consumed with shaky fingers after the hotel lost power. I remember running my little fingers along the seams of my booster seat for forgotten raisins or bits of cereal. Nothing.

When the rain subsided enough, and some guys with chainsaws cut up some big trees on the road, we parked the car, which seemed more like a boat now, near the only place that had lights on in the town. A generator, my mother guessed, was fueling the diner-like building. It was not the kind of place where we usually ate. The linoleum floors were covered with muddy shoe prints, bits of grass, and tiny bits of gravel drug in by patrons. A plump, rosy-cheeked lady with a pastel uniform and grease-stained white apron made eye-contact with us when the door jingled as we entered. The air was thick and smelled like a gym; people packed together like they were waiting for something—the last flight out or a spiritual leader's blessing.

Everyone crammed into vinyl-covered booths. Greetings were murmured. Periodically people looked out the fogged-up, smudged glass windows like children warily eyeing a snarling dog moving away from them.

The waitress distributed stacks of pancakes. A girl with pink hair passed me a box of plastic forks with the care one might devote to the collection plate at church.

Somebody laughed. Somebody drew a smile on the window. Somebody prayed out loud. The overhead lights shined, steadily.

Judy Childs
NO DIFFERENT

I can't breathe. I'm lying facedown in the dry, sun-soaked field, after Ella and Max—120 pounds of glorious dog power—have stampeded me. They sounded like horses galloping up behind me, but I continued my walk in the field unconcerned. They never run into me, until today. I think I'm dying. I am alone, and the sun sits low on the horizon. Ella and Max are off again to dance, wrestle, and collide like mountain goats. I live, limp home, and a broken rib slices every breath I take.

  I am still hurting a month later, but Ella and I meet Amy for a hike by the Boardman River. We cross the Union Street Bridge to return to the downtown parking lot. Ella, my sweet, gazelle-like black lab puppy, walks next to Amy. West Bay shimmers in the hot sun that burns the top of our heads. Glancing under the bridge, I see a comatose, homeless man sprawled out on a stone ledge. A friend is with him, pulling on his hand. I look away. Seeing this man totally incapacitated disturbs me, but I forget it quickly. I have seen drunken homeless folks before.

  The parking lot is busy in August, and a quick motion back by the trees draws my eye. A snarling, nasty mutt bolts away from his owner and lunges at my sweet Ella. He growls, jumps, and bites Ella on her back. The whites of Ella's eyes show as she rolls her eyes back to see this monster. She yips, wrenches out of her collar, and takes off; Amy is left holding an empty leash. I call Ella, but she races by me with a look that says, "Forget it." I'm a wreck: new knee, torn rotator cuff, and fractured rib. Ella gallops smoothly in large circles in the parking lot. Her fear is palpable. The attacker snaps, spits, and growls, but he can't catch up. I love my girl but cannot help her. Amy yells and throws her shoes at the mangy mutt. Sick with fear, I watch the cars race by on the parkway.

  A young man appears; he's running and waving his arms at Ella. He wears a red bandana with a long, brown ponytail, and he lunges and dives at Ella. He misses. He kicks his sandals off and pursues Ella hard. His sunglasses fly off. He crouches, a wide-legged stance, arms out, like he's guarding her in basketball. As cars zoom by, the young man dives again and captures Ella in a bear hug. She tries to break free from her savior, and I run over to join him in a dog hug to restrain Ella. I face him at arm's length. Beneath the red bandana, a beaming face, scruffy beard, and smiling brown eyes meet me. I melt in gratitude for this sweet man, but think that he must be the bad dog's owner.

"Hi. I'm Judy. What's your name?" I ask, heart pounding, amazed that I can even speak.

"Randy."

"Hi Randy, Your dog bit my dog." He looks puzzled. "Is that dog yours?"

"No."

I lean in to grasp Ella tighter as she fights to break free, and I'm so very close to this guy. Ella is sandwiched between us.

"I'm kind of close here, Randy," I smile.

"That's ok," he smiles back.

I'm practically in this guy's lap, but I feel a sweetness and openness that touches me. My life is this moment, this tiny space; everything else is a blur. Randy looks directly into my eyes as he talks to me. He's comfortable with who he is. Ella is terrified and continues to struggle. We chat about Ella and her MSU collar; we both went to MSU. Randy was in engineering; I was in education.

"Do you live in town?" I continue chatting. Ella is finally calming down.

"I'm homeless," he states.

My eyebrows crinkle and my eyes drop. How could this strong, clean, good-to-the-bone young man be homeless? I see his broken sunglasses on the ground.

"I broke my sunglasses," he says.

"I'll buy you new ones."

"I promise to spend this on sunglasses."

He really is homeless. How can this hero be homeless? He looks like one of my friends. No different.

Amy runs over and fastens the collar on Ella. Randy mildly accepts my profuse thanks, gathers his sandals, broken sunglasses, and leaves. I don't want him to go. Amy is shaking. We walk to her car and Amy hugs me tight, sobbing.

"That dog was terrifying," she says.

"I know."

"Is Ella ok?

"I don't know.

"And he's homeless. How does that even happen?"

There's a lot I don't know. Now a homeless man has saved my Ella. He put a face on those who struggle while putting himself in harm's way to save a frightened puppy. Randy saw something wrong, and he made it right. There is something pure about him.

I've always judged homeless people without even realizing it—just averted my eyes and walked away. Now, I want to know more: how do people become homeless? What is a day like for them? How do they survive a night? I run into a friend the next night and tell her of the man who saved Ella, and that I want to volunteer with people in need. Janie, also a retired teacher, says, "Hey! I know where you can volunteer—at a writing workshop for street people. They write for Speak Up, Traverse City's street newspaper."

Three days later I am in the United Way building, walking down the long, twisting hall to the workshop. People are gathered in the kitchen getting a meal ready. Entering quietly, I stand at the end of the counter. There is Randy. He sees me and smiles. He's the only person I know.

"Hi! Did you know that I'd be here?"

"No, but I am happy to see you." I pull a thank you card from my purse and slide it over to him. I had a feeling I would see him again. The others welcome me, and we all join in a meal like one big happy family. Then we discuss prompts, write, share, smile, and nod. This chaotic, sweet group becomes my new writing group.

And Randy? He is my friend.

Phillip Sterling
CALL ME MAXIE!

Although it was clearly not the house for us, Richard had the presence of mind to be both fanciful and meticulous. He'd gone out to take one more look around the property, leaving me in the kitchen with the realtor.

But I had seen enough. It was the fourth open house we had visited that afternoon, and somewhere among the three-to-four bedrooms, Jacuzzi tubs, and gently sloping lawns, I'd apparently lost my "spirit of adventure," as Richard called it, which resulted in the distinctive qualities of the first three properties melding into less than memorable variations on a theme, like Monet's paintings of the ponds at Giverny. I'd told Richard he was more than welcome to take last look around, but I had reached the point in our house hunting where suffering the inevitable pitch of a salesperson would be preferable to debating where in the yard the swing set—*if* we were to have kids someday—might go. Which is how I came to be seated on a stool beside the island in the kitchen.

Fortunately, the realtor—*Call me Maxie!* read the business cards scattered on the gray-flecked Corian in front of me)—didn't appear interested in small talk. For several minutes she ignored me, focusing her attention instead on the phone she cupped in both hands and jabbed at, left and right, with her thumbs—as if the device were some kind of digital sparring partner. While dressed the part of a broker's agent—a tight-fitting peach-colored skirt and blouse offset by a silver-threaded, lime-green scarf—*Call-me-Maxie!* slouched against the counter near the sink with nonchalance atypical of the realtors we'd met thus far.

I was grateful for the inattention at first, thinking, *Just a moment's rest.* But as the disregard lengthened, I began to feel a little uneasy, like when you're riding a slow elevator with a stranger in a wet bathing suit. By the time the woman did speak, I wasn't sure if she was addressing me or someone on the phone.

"Wha'dya think?" she said.

"I'm sorry?"

Call-me-Maxie! waved her phone through the air as if she were a fairy godmother with a magic wand. "The house," she said, indicating.

"It's nice," I replied, modulating my voice to emphasize nice, hoping the curt ambiguity of my answer would be sufficient.

The agent's right index finger began flicking the face of her phone, frantically, as if trying to dissuade an insect intent on pollinating her email. "The only comparable," she said, "is over on Bayberry. Twenty-one-hundred-square-feet—but just one-and-a half baths, and no island in the kitchen." Her right arm swung open, her flat-palmed hand signifying the window above the farmhouse sink. "No view," she said. "No yard to speak of." Her gesture brought to mind reruns of *The Price Is Right*; she could have doubled as a game show model.

"I think we've seen that one," I said, to dispel her sales pitch. But to be honest I wasn't sure.

"What's your husband think?"

The question caught me off guard.

"He's not my husband," I admitted. "At least not yet. We're planning a wedding for sometime next year."

For several seconds the woman stared at me, coldly. Her lips, slick with purplish gloss—a garish contrast to the green scarf—parted slightly, as if she were about to say something but then had second thoughts. The look was disconcerting, even accusative. In response, I cast my sight out the window above the sink, where gauzy wisps of clouds tangled in the treetops. I wondered how much longer Richard would be.

"Congratulations," said the woman, flatly. She returned her attention to her phone. "The name's Maxie, if you have any questions."

The dismissal was obvious. It unnerved me even more than her initial disregard. At first, I felt the need to explain, to tell her how house hunting had been Richard's idea—to get started early, even though our wedding was months away. Although he'd only been employed by NB Financial for eighteen months—68% of which we'd been dating (he'd pointed out)—Richard had received two promotions already, with salary bonuses sufficient enough to set aside a small down payment for a house of our own. *So we may as well start looking,* he'd said, when we'd gone out to dinner to celebrate his most recent promotion. It was that night—over shared tiramisu—I'd agreed to become Richard's wife.

Yet none of that, I decided, was something a complete stranger, realtor or not, needed to know.

"Maple syrup," said Maxie suddenly.

"I'm sorry?" Again, I wasn't sure if she was talking to the phone or me.

"The jar on the windowsill," said Maxie, lifting her heavy eyes to look my way. "Everybody asks about it. I thought maybe you were just too shy. It's the last jar from the year of their divorce. The owner's ex was serious about sugaring. He bought the place, she said, for the trees."

"The jar on the window—"

I'd been staring right past it, thinking about Richard. That's how tired I was. But now that it was pointed out, I don't know how I could have missed the quart-sized canning jar above the sink. It positively glowed, with the sun coming in from behind.

"It goes with the house," continued Maxie. "The seller found it in the basement when she was cleaning—thought the new owners might like it since it came from the trees on the property. Her ex left it behind—the *only* thing he'd left behind, *besides her*—she'd said."

"It's lovely," I said. More amber than gold, the liquid in the jar glimmered transparently.

"I once had a pair of earrings that color," said Maxie. She looked up from her phone and toward the window. "*Amber* earrings. My second husband brought the stones back from Poland—he'd gone there on business—had them mounted at S&G Jewelers here in town. They were like tiny silver fish nets with amber pearls inside—almost that same color."

"Really," I said. I couldn't help it—I looked at her ears. What at first seemed to be silver crosses dangling from her lobes were in fact small For Sale signs with the word *Sold* engraved across the top.

"I could have had a ring made," she continued, "but I wanted something to complement my dress, which was off-white . . . *second* wedding, and all that. They were a perfect match. Hard to find maple syrup that light these days. I think commercial producers must add coloring or something to make it all look the same."

"That'd be my guess too," I said, to let her know I was listening. She'd returned to swiping at her phone.

The color *was* intriguing—nothing like what I think of as maple syrup, which is darker, more caramel. The only liquid I'd ever seen similar in color to the jar above the sink was one or another of the craft beers Richard ordered, occasionally, when we went out.

And where was Richard now?

"The USDA syrup grading system," Maxie said, "uses five different maple grades, according to Maple Source dot com." She read from her phone: "'Three graded A—Grade A Light Amber, Grade A Medium Amber, Grade A Dark Amber—and two darker syrups—Grade B maple syrup and Commercial Grade. These grades have specific and important upper and lower limits for color and flavor. Grade A Light Amber has a very delicate maple flavor. Medium Amber has a nice mild flavor. Grade A Dark Amber has a full-bodied maple flavor while Grade B—including Grade B organic maple syrup—has a hearty, robust flavor.' All are great on pancakes and waffles, it says, but the extra flavor in Grade A Dark Amber and Grade B maple syrup allow these two to be of great use as cooking ingredients as well."

"Really?" I said.

"Nothing about molasses. But I'm guessing that the jar on the sill is probably Medium Amber—based on the examples pictured here—the same color as my earrings."

"Huh," I said, in my best *that's-interesting* voice. Then aloud: "I wonder what's keeping him."

"*Honey,*" said Maxie, lifting her head enough to look my way, "trust me. It's better you didn't know." Once again, she returned her attention to the phone.

I wasn't sure what she'd meant, but fairly certain she didn't have Richard in mind. If anything, Richard was more Golden Retriever—the kind of dog he'd said would be good with kids—than one of the gray mixed-breed rescues my family kept when I was growing up, the kind of wandering, garbage-routing dogs neighbors sometimes complained about.

"*PO*-lish amber," Maxie continued, reading from her phone, "also known as *Gold of the North*, is the most valuable type of amber. Its rich, honey-like structure makes this Baltic treasure a genuine piece of art. Amber jewelry produced by the best manufacturers of the city of...*jee-dans-kee*...reveals the natural beauty of Baltic...*B*-something—spelled b-u-r-s-z-t-y-n—which means *burning stone*. Designers bring its genuine beauty back into life in unique and stylish pieces of jewelry."

"It's pronounced *G*-dansk," I said, emphasizing the hard G. Although it probably hadn't been more than a few minutes, my time with *Call-me-Maxie!* was beginning to feel interminable—the afternoon draining into darkness, the sunlight fading. The color of the syrup on the windowsill appeared to have grown more deeply orange, even reddish, since it was first drawn to my attention, tending toward what I imagined Maxie would say was as Grade A Dark syrup or even Grade B. I could see in the distance beyond the jar, beyond the sun-tipped trees lining the yard—likely maples, it occurred to me—the clouds' white wisps had sullied into gray.

"I bought it at a consignment store," Maxie said. "My dress. A kind of damask, I thought, off-white. I mean, it was not the first rodeo, you know. The earrings went perfectly."

"I can imagine," I said. And what I imagined was a dingy, late-19th Century wedding photo processed in sepia, the whole thing tinted brown, as if it had been recovered from a flooded basement.

"Retail prices for maple syrup," said the realtor, "are currently higher than anticipated. The average locations across the U.S. sold maple syrup for about $96.50 per gallon. Of course, this was mostly in smaller units, making the out-of-pocket cost seem more reasonable. The average unit size for the cheapest maple syrup was 18.8 ounces, which means that the average unit sold was smaller than that. In the face of short supply, it says here, many retailers sold smaller units at higher prices, and this may have accounted for the increase."

She paused as if for a response, but I had none.

"Kind of like real estate," she said, glaring, which gave me no choice but to reply.

"I wouldn't know," I said. "We've just begun to look."

Maxie shifted from one leg to another, bowed again to her phone. All at once the smell of careless hygiene and unwashed clothes seem to override the vanilla-scented candle that, I noticed, no longer burned on the coil-less stove top. I began to wonder if maybe I should go looking for Richard. Maybe something happened to him; maybe he'd gotten lost in the 2.6 wooded acres.

"It's the same with amber," said Maxie, "according to this other website. Baltic amber jewelry is particularly valued. Amber stones fetch a good price in the global market. They make wonderful gifts, it says."

"Really." The word was becoming my mantra.

"'The early Germans called Baltic amber by the name of *Bernstein*,'" read Maxie, "'due to the sweet smell it emitted when burnt. The Greeks called it *Elektron* due to its properties of developing static electricity when rubbed. Amber is known as *Kerba* in the local markets in India' . . .

"And this is interesting," she continued, "amber gemstone was believed to possess magical power, since it was warm to touch, light weight, produced static electricity when rubbed and smelled sweet when heated. Wearing amber as an amulet was highly recommended to safeguard the wearer from evil and from negative energy."

"Really?" I said emphatically, once again, praying that the door would soon open and Richard would appear—. At that moment, I wished I'd had an amber amulet of my own.

"*Safeguard*, my ass," said Maxie bitterly, her tone of voice dropping two shades darker than the syrup on the windowsill, which had browned to the color of a taffeta gown under a too hot iron.

"*Sorry?*"

"It was a good thing I didn't spend the money on a new dress," the realtor said, tossing her phone with a kind of careless disdain onto the pile of property descriptions and disclosers that lay before me. "We weren't married three months before that cheating S-O-B decided that the earrings would look better on someone else. Left me with just the crummy second-hand dress—which, as I said, *matched perfectly*."

She was staring in my direction with an intensity that would have been frightening if I'd thought it was about me. But I wasn't even there. She was looking right through me, or right past—the way I had overlooked the jar of maple syrup on the windowsill.

The moment was disturbing, chilling—though not in the way you would expect it to be, not like in the movies when the heroine realizes she is trapped in a haunted house with a psychopath. I didn't feel afraid or vulnerable. Instead, I felt a chill of recognition. "I'm sorry," I said again. And I meant it.

"I thought I could still salvage something," Maxie said. "I thought I could still get some use out of the dress. I mean, it was second-hand but not cheap. Perhaps if it had been a different color, perhaps if it was burgundy . . . Well, the dress dyed horribly, being polyester, and so I threw it on the burn pile with the clothes he'd left behind . . ."

I had nothing left to say I suddenly wanted to go. I wanted to be somewhere else, and yet, just as suddenly, I was no longer in any hurry for Richard to take me wherever somewhere else was. I began to wonder if maybe I should call an Uber—or even ask *Call-me-Maxie!* for a ride. Surely the Open House would be over soon. The glow of the syrup on the windowsill had faded in the late afternoon sun.

Maxie's phone began to buzz. She picked it up and glanced at whatever text or number was displayed there, then turned back to me. "This can all be yours," she said, waving her phone through the space between us, "Just make an offer."

William Palmer
AT NORTH PEAK BREWING

I see a couple at a table
in their sixties,
not talking much.

He leans in
as if listening
to a favorite song.

Her back is straight,
her gray hair pulled back.
She watches a waitress place
a dark beer and a light beer
before a young couple whose voices
spark the air—they don't think
about their talk going dry
like a riverbed.

Before they leave, she goes
to the restroom.

He stands,
looking at the tall silver tanks
where fermentation happens
hidden. He sees the pressure dials.

Christine Rhein
AT THE DETROIT INSTITUTE OF ARTS

Long ago, on our second date—you,
a skinny guy fresh from Kansas City,

suggested we visit the museum, and I—
Detroit girl of 22—had to confess

that I'd never been to it before.
A brand-new pair of auto engineers,

we started out—by chance—
at the Rivera murals, assembly lines

running in front and back of us
that Saturday afternoon. I remember,

in the next gallery, how you tried out
your German—*Ritter* and *Rüstüng*—

knight and armor—the gleaming
shields and helmets making us laugh

about Monty Python, silly quests.
I studied the map, while you delighted

in getting us lost. And now, here we stand,
side by side, once again, taking in the art

we've grown to call our favorites—
our green-glazed Pewabic vase,

and the peasants in *The Wedding Dance*—
their awkward lustfulness, red-hued frenzy.

And last—like always—the nocturne,
Whistler asking us to study the dark

canvas, the flecks of gold—falling
sparks—fireworks in the fog.

Erica Photiades
THE WATCH

I bought my father a watch for his sixty-fifth birthday. Not just any watch, but a Shinola watch, made in Detroit. The Shinola company is a consumerist phoenix: the rebirth of an American ideal that all goods are better if they are made here, and even better if they are made in Detroit. The repurposed product has no connection to the long-defunct Shinola shoe polish; just a name floating in the suspended animation of failed businesses like a dead man's social security number. With some inventive rebranding, a company can create a new corporate mythology from whatever tropes tick the boxes of *Freedom! Resilience! Made in America!* The original tagline, "You don't know shit from Shinola," was resurrected as the perfect origin story for luxury watches. And Detroit? The city needed to build something again.

The idea of buying a Shinola watch came to me when my father mailed me a full-page color advertisement for Shinola products that ran in *The New York Times.* My dad likes to send me newspaper articles he thinks would interest me. He scrawls messages across the margins in pen, *"Look at what is happening in Detroit!"* The clean lines of his angular handwriting are reminiscent of a Frank Lloyd Wright blueprint, adding his personal foreword to a news story about the revitalization of an abandoned masterpiece of twentieth century architecture downtown, or a clipping from the sports page full of sincere optimism for the Lions' football season. This time, his message above the sleek advertisement was, *"You could get me one of these for my birthday."*

As a homesick Midwesterner stuck in Waco, Texas, I looked forward to my father's hopeful missives, saving each one of his letters like they were rare artifacts of anthropological significance that living in the land of Southern Baptists and barbecue seemed all too eager to erase from my past. If I touched newsprint from back home, I could remember Michigan winters; the way the color of melting snow in the streets was the same gray as the paper, endlessly sluiced onto the sidewalks by cars rushing past. I kept his letters because I missed standing in my parents' kitchen, watching him perform basic tasks like jotting down a grocery list on the counter.

As my years in Texas accumulated, running my fingers across his handwriting sometimes felt like the closest we would ever be again.

Texas doesn't have defined seasons, which gives it the feeling that time has stopped. There are seemingly unending periods of furnace-blasting heat coupled with malarial humidity, and then one morning, you wake to a slight chill in the air and see all the leaves have wilted off the trees like salad gone bad in the fridge. That's what passes for fall. One October day, as I was talking to my dad on the phone, I admitted that I missed seeing the leaves change color. He went outside to the curb, collected a pile of maple leaves that had fallen into the street, and mailed them to me. I kept the leaves until they turned brown and crumbled into dust.

It has always been difficult to buy gifts for my father. He is appreciative but picky if an item is not of his specific choosing. I have inherited this trait as well. Yes, I like books, but why should I like this particular book kind of thing. A newspaper clipping requesting a Shinola watch seemed like a clear signal that I could finally give him a gift he would treasure. I eagerly jumped on their website to research options, only to balk at how much a Shinola watch cost. The entry-level model rang in at $650. The options for customization were overwhelming. There were different color watch faces, face diameter, and leather bands. I had to get everything right.

Every gift is a form of nostalgia, in its way. I chose a watch face of forest green because it was the same color as my dad's 1973 Fiat Spyder, an inexpensive but stylish Italian sports car with its own mythology in the pantheon of my family's gods. My father's Fiat has had many rhetorical renovations during the fifty years he has owned it; once a chariot for wooing sweethearts, it most recently became his transportation of choice to carry him into the underworld. But that's a story for another time.

I grew up riding in the Fiat for every special occasion from school dances to my wedding. Every summer, our family cruised Woodward Avenue, the first concrete road built in the state, connecting the city of Detroit to its northern suburbs. My younger brother and I squeezed ourselves into the Fiat's cramped backseat, no seatbelts, while my father took the vinyl top down and placed his arm around my mother's shoulder. Woodward Avenue is so ubiquitous to the origin story of the Motor City that Detroit and its suburbs hold a classic car festival called the Dream Cruise every August to commemorate the chrome-plated glory days of the city. My father was on the original planning committee for this event.

For a weekend that often stretches into an entire month, the streets of Detroit fill with the leonine roar of eight-cylinder engines, the humid, late summer air clogged with lead-tinged exhaust at levels that would make any environmentalist clutch their proverbial pearls. Woodward Avenue becomes an assembly line of Detroit's history as the parade of vintage cars rolls down the road chronologically; Model Ts puttering along first, followed by sequential decades until finally the 1970s arrive and my father's Fiat is proudly revving past with the other foreign sports cars. It is like witnessing the heart of a great industrial beast pump automobiles into the veins of America. I spent a lot of time pondering my childhood memories as I researched the best way to memorialize my father's life in a watch.

I wanted to add a personalized engraving to accompany his gift. My dad loved the original *Twilight Zone* television series, and we spent many nights during my childhood watching a black-and-white-striped circle spin into the abyss of space as Rod Serling's voice announced, "You are traveling through another dimension, not only of sight and sound but of mind. Your next stop...The Twilight Zone." My father's favorite episode was about an isolated, harried man played by actor Burgess Meredith who survives a nuclear blast. His despair turns to joy as he rushes to the decimated library, reaching for the books scattered around the detritus. "I have time now! All the time in the world!" he exclaims, before his glasses fall from his face and shatter on the ground. My dad repeated the actor's final whimpering line, "That's not fair!" whenever we recalled the scene together. I arranged to have the title of the episode, "Time Enough at Last," embossed on the underside of the leather watch band.

The watch arrived in a wooden box with the Shinola label stamped on the top, placed on a pedestal to rival the Hope Diamond's. Inside was a handwritten card signed by the woman who built the watch in Detroit's Shinola factory. On my dad's birthday in May, I wrote him a poem that cleverly hinted at the gift he would receive when I visited Michigan later that summer. I told my mother what I had planned, and when my dad received my letter, she told me, "Well, he liked the poem, but he has no idea what it means."

In July, I made the 1,400-mile drive from Texas to Michigan, eager to deliver the watch. When I presented him with his gift, his expression was a familiar one. His thick black eyebrows rose and he said, "Oh!" in the way he always does when he is unsure of how to respond. I have inherited this trait as well: a Pandora's Box of feelings that opens across my face when there is no clear direction how I should react to a situation. My father's thoughtful expression deepened the wrinkles in his face as he absorbed the promise of future time in its beautiful wooden box. My mother took the lead on delivering emotional gravitas to the moment. She pulled me into the hallway and burst into tears.

"The city never gave him a watch when he left. All those years he worked, he just wanted something to say thank you."

It had been four years since his beloved employer removed him from being its Public Works Director, stripped him of dignity and forced him into retirement without even a cheap sheet cake to commemorate his forty years of service. He began his career as a hopeful twenty-one-year-old supervising a city ice skating rink, moving up the ranks until he ran a city department, and ended it a broken man choosing suicide in his Fiat of British Racing Green, closing the garage door one gray March day and letting the pre-catalytic converter engine run as his lungs breathed in the poison of his past. Much like Burgess Meredith's plight in "Time Enough at Last," my father's career ended in a pile of rubble, his professional accomplishments lost to the exhaust of time.

While the watch was not meant to be a reminder of this betrayal, an impressive timepiece made in Detroit could recall those darker times as a symbol of the recognition my father's employer denied him. I was acutely aware of the time I sometimes felt we had stolen, because he didn't die that day. Our neighbor heard the Fiat running in the garage and called 911. The fire department broke down the door, saving his life. My father lived to celebrate his sixty-fifth birthday, where I gave him his Shinola watch. There are many timelines that could have denied us this moment, and I am grateful that we get to have this one. As my father continues to add memories to the coda of his life, I remind myself that time itself is a gift, and never one we can depend on.

80

The watch stopped working six months after I gave it to him. Despite Shinola's assurance that it was engineered with the highest quality, it failed at the job it was built to do. My father drove to Detroit's Shinola factory to have it repaired, and as an apology, the company let him replace it with any watch he wanted. He now has one with a larger face and a background of blue like a partly cloudy sky. He wears it every day, its mechanics as reliable as the pulse of his own heart underneath them. So far, it has not failed him.

The watch continues to evolve as a symbol in my father's life. It is more than a birthday gift, the rebirth of Detroit, his career, the Fiat, *The Twilight Zone*. A chronicle of future memories to be made while it continues to keep time for all of us. A metaphor for time in all its shapes and colors and dimensions. A storytelling device that Rod Serling would have appreciated, had he been standing off to the side, smoking the cigarettes that would eventually kill him, devising a poignant narrative to break the fourth wall to the scene we are living in.

"Our story opens on the Photiades family, a reunion where their daughter has returned from Texas, bearing the gift of a watch for her father on his sixty-fifth birthday. A watch made in Detroit, with a face the color of memories. The memories of forty years past, but also the memory of a death delayed. A timepiece for our time, delivered here, in the Twilight Zone."

Calvin VanErgens
PANTOUM FOR A WEEK AT PARADISE HOLLOW

The gift of precious time and losing track of time
'til wafts of charcoal grill smoke signals supper's soon.
Then sitting fireside later on, we'll want S'mores.
Recalling childhood, savor sweet and sticky joy.

'Til wafts of charcoal grill smoke signals supper's soon,
sit only watching. That will be enough, so watch,
recalling childhood. Savor sweet and sticky joy,
the wind in clapping leaves so full of quiet hush.

Sit only watching. That will be enough, so watch
the open water filling depths and spreading flat,
the wind in clapping leaves so full of quiet hush
and hollow eerie music that loons cry out —

the open waters, filling depths and spreading flat,
that carry both the cannonballers' raucous shouts
and hollow eerie music that loons cry out.
My heart and lungs keep drumming rhythmic songs of rest

that carry both the cannonballer's raucous shouts
and drifting mind with poised expectant line and lure.
My heart and lungs keep drumming rhythmic songs of rest
with bass that surges low and strong within their depths

and drifting mind with poised expectant line and lure.
The minnows form a river, swift within the lake
with bass that surges low and strong within their depths.
The rippled water shimmers with the sun. Fish,

the minnows, form a river, swift within the lake
and darting here and there, avoiding lakeside guests.
The rippled water shimmers with the sunfish
as briefly they are lifted, dancing, from their lives.

And darting here and there, avoiding, lakeside guests
become at home inside this little piece of North,
as briefly they are lifted, dancing from their lives.
As if this wasn't living, patterned through their years.

Become at home inside this little piece of North,
returning here, this place your reminiscence lives.
As if this wasn't living. Patterned through their years,
the rest of life, a rhythm more than daily grind

returning here, this place. Your reminiscence lives
then, sitting fireside. Later on, we'll want some more,
the rest—of life, a rhythm more than daily grind:
the gift of precious time and losing track of time.

Joan Donaldson
SAND

My broom whispered back and forth across the soft pine flooring, clearing away the sand my gritty toes had deposited during the day. Over seven decades, bare feet had tracked in enough of Lake Michigan's sand to smooth the cottage's floorboards to a golden patina. My broom brushed a scattering of pine needles and bits of brown oak leaves that littered the back porch, but sand was the main sediment.

"It's good clean beach sand. It never harmed anyone," my employer, Miss Bartow, said as I swept the sand out the porch door. Considering I only donned sandals to ride my bike into town to pick up the mail, I was grateful that Miss Bartow shared the same attitude about sandy bare feet.

"Before we could string a clothesline between a couple of trees, we draped our washing over shrubs. If they dragged onto the sand, we just brushed it off when the clothes dried."

Miss Bartow sat on her sunporch with a book in her lap, her gray head bowed. The gold beads around her neck shimmered in the slanted rays of the sun setting over Lake Michigan. Now and then, she gazed at the waves through thick glasses that magnified her blue eyes. In 1898 when she was three, her parents had built this cottage. Back then, only tufts of beach grass and a few oak saplings clung to the dunes.

Thousands of years ago, when the glaciers ruled the north, those great icy eels slid south from Canada. The giant eels slithered over a mass of granite that covered three million square miles, from eastern Canada into the Northwest. Gravel and rocks encrusted the bellies of the glaciers which scraped across the earth, carving rocks that form the Lake Michigan basin. When warm winds breathed on the icy monsters, they writhed, and water trickled from their pores. Their bodies flung sand and gravel into hills called glacial moraines that formed a barrier at the edge of the lake and dammed the water filling the basin. When high winds and waves crashed into the dirt wall, they scoured sand from the moraines, and lake currents carried these sediments, depositing them along the shoreline. Storm after storm, the sand dunes grew.

Every afternoon, I lounged on Miss Bartow's beach along with our neighbor, Mrs. Gielow, and her two young daughters and son. With plastic shovels, her children scooped wet sand into small buckets and dumped the contents into a lumpy ring that formed a sandcastle. They dug a narrow trench around the fort and excavated a channel to the lake, sending water into their moat. Sand coated their legs and arms. They abandoned their sculpture to frolic in the waves which reclaimed the sand from their bodies.

A gust of wind lifted sand and flung it across my body. I licked the grit from my lips, tasting eons of smashed rocks. I raced into the waves and floated on my back, staring up at the same blue sky that had witnessed the glaciers. Soon, I trudged up the stairs scaling the incline that led to Miss Bartow's cottage, perched like an acorn beneath a circle of red oak trees. The screen door swooshed behind me; my toes and ankles scattered a faint trail of sand into my bedroom.

One evening, I examined the different shapes and colors of the grains of sand in my dustpan and recognized minerals I had studied in my geology classes. Bits of clear quartz, white and pink feldspar, and black hematite sparkled in the sunlight. Ancient particles of granite freed by Lake Michigan as the waves rolled pebbles along the shore.

Mrs. Gielow drove her car along a winding narrow tarmac that curved through the dunes, while Miss Bartow rode shot gun and chattered about the weather. Every morning, I pedaled this route on my way to the village of Douglas. But sitting in the back seat of a car offered a less tactile encounter with the blue chicory flowers and the goldfinches flitting about a cottage's lilac bushes. Finally, we turned onto a driveway with a sign: The Singapore Yacht Club, and we parked near a low, rectangular gray-sided building.

"Why is the yacht club named after Singapore?" I asked.

"Because in the mid-1800s, the town of Singapore was settled at the mouth of the river," Miss Bartow answered. "The sand dunes buried it."

In the 1830s, Oshea Wilder, a wealthy man from New York, established the settlement named Singapore at the mouth of the Kalamazoo River. Eventually, he sold the land to other investors,

Every afternoon, I lounged on Miss Bartow's beach along with our neighbor, Mrs. Gielow, and her two young daughters and son. With plastic shovels, her children scooped wet sand into small buckets and dumped the contents into a lumpy ring that formed a sandcastle. They dug a narrow trench around the fort and excavated a channel to the lake, sending water into their moat. Sand coated their legs and arms. They abandoned their sculpture to frolic in the waves which reclaimed the sand from their bodies.

A gust of wind lifted sand and flung it across my body. I licked the grit from my lips, tasting eons of smashed rocks. I raced into the waves and floated on my back, staring up at the same blue sky that had witnessed the glaciers. Soon, I trudged up the stairs scaling the incline that led to Miss Bartow's cottage, perched like an acorn beneath a circle of red oak trees. The screen door swooshed behind me; my toes and ankles scattered a faint trail of sand into my bedroom.

One evening, I examined the different shapes and colors of the grains of sand in my dustpan and recognized minerals I had studied in my geology classes. Bits of clear quartz, white and pink feldspar, and black hematite sparkled in the sunlight. Ancient particles of granite freed by Lake Michigan as the waves rolled pebbles along the shore.

Mrs. Gielow drove her car along a winding narrow tarmac that curved through the dunes, while Miss Bartow rode shot gun and chattered about the weather. Every morning, I pedaled this route on my way to the village of Douglas. But sitting in the back seat of a car offered a less tactile encounter with the blue chicory flowers and the goldfinches flitting about a cottage's lilac bushes. Finally, we turned onto a driveway with a sign: The Singapore Yacht Club, and we parked near a low, rectangular gray-sided building.

"Why is the yacht club named after Singapore?" I asked.

"Because in the mid-1800s, the town of Singapore was settled at the mouth of the river," Miss Bartow answered. "The sand dunes buried it."

In the 1830s, Oshea Wilder, a wealthy man from New York, established the settlement named Singapore at the mouth of the Kalamazoo River. Eventually, he sold the land to other investors, who eyed the thick stands of white pine and hardwood trees blanketing the low dunes, and they calculated the board feet hidden beneath the trees' bark. By the 1850s, Singapore boasted two sawmills, a wildcat bank, several general stores, and two hotels, plus boarding houses and homes for the lumbermen, sawmill employees, and shipbuilders.

The sounds of axes and saws, and the crash of trees striking the earth rippled along the lakeshore. Teamsters shouted at their horses as they drove wagonloads of logs to the sawmills where large round blades whined and sliced the ancient trees. The scent of sawdust drifted through the town. Historians estimate that Singapore's mills cut over three million board feet each year.

Near the wharf, shipwrights hammered some of the planking into schooners, such as the Octavia, which transported lumber to Chicago. Teams of oxen hauled the straightest and tallest pine trees to the docks and men resurrected them as masts. Just as a man's thinning hair exposes a bald spot on his head, in sections of the dunes, the sunlight illuminated shimmering sand.

During the summer of 1871, a blazing sun toasted Chicago and little rain fell. Over two-thirds of the city's houses, factories, and shops were built from wood, and even wooden planks formed the sidewalks. Folklore suggests that on October 8th, Mrs. O'Leary's cow kicked over a lantern that lit her barn on fire. From that farmyard on the southwest side of town, waves of fire swept north and east into the heart of Chicago, burning a strip one mile wide and four miles long. Over 17,500 buildings succumbed to the conflagration, leaving thousands homeless.

Chicago coveted wood. The giant city opened its maw and screamed for millions of boards. The Singapore sawmill owners brought in more lumbermen. A cacophony of axes, crosscut saws, and the endless screeching of the sawmills filled the air. Heavy boots trampled wildflowers which were soon covered by woodchips. Tree after tree crashed to the earth, leaving only stumps and withering roots.

The gales of November blasted the sand away from twisted tree roots. Winds shoved the grains, and they tumbled down the slope. At first, the sand inched towards Singapore, but with no plants or grass to hinder movement, the dunes soon slid up to ten feet per year. Sand covered the first stories of houses and seeped into the hotels and stores. The businessmen tore apart the sawmills and shipped them to the forests in the Upper Peninsula of Michigan. Singapore's residents packed their trunks and followed the mills north or traipsed inland for work at the Douglas Basket factory. When frigid temperatures froze the Kalamazoo River, teams of horses dragged the bank building and several houses to Saugatuck. Eventually, the dunes smothered Singapore.

One spring afternoon, a friend and I wandered north from Miss Bartow's cottage on a path that ran along the top of the sand dunes. "Miss Bartow called this the bear path and said that the Native Americans created it. Supposedly, it starts farther south of her cottage," I explained. "I assume she referred to the Potawatomi who once lived here."

We lost the path when walking through a cluster of cottages known as Shorewood. But on the other side of the summer community, we spied the faint trail that led us through woods dotted by clouds of creamy juneberry blossoms. Our feet crushed the blades of grass extending through the brown thatch of last year's growth. At the edge of a meadow, we walked into the ball diamond belonging to the Presbyterian Camps where inner-city youth could escape Chicago for a week of fresh air.

"I think the camp covers the trail," I said to my friend. We ran down a footpath to the beach, shrieking as we stuck our feet in the frigid water. Our walk along the shoreline ended at the Saugatuck pier which protected the mouth of the Kalamazoo River. A few fishermen stood on the cement wall, casting their lines into the low waves. I gazed across the dunes to where Singapore's sawmill once screamed.

"Rest in peace," I whispered to the memories buried beneath the sand.

Nineteenth century avarice destroyed an ecosystem. But over the coming years, birds dropped seeds that sprouted into tall clumps of grass, juneberry bushes, and a few sumac trees. Their roots stabilized the inner ridges of dunes, but when the water levels in Lake Michigan rose, the waves carved into the lip of sand closest to the shoreline. In a few places, cottage owners littered the dunes with slabs of cement, but the Lake laughed and tossed the chunks like pebbles.

One hot summer day, billionaire Aubrey McClendon, the Fracking King and founder of Chesapeake Energy, zoomed along the Saugatuck shoreline on his jet ski. Just north of the mouth of the Kalamazoo River, he observed acres of rolling sand dunes dotted with a few scrubby Scotch pine trees and waving grass. A couple of hikers walked a maze of paths leading to the beach, but McClendon didn't see any cottages, nor did he know how these dunes hid Singapore.

McClendon had spotted the land known to the locals as the Denison Property, named after the family who owned it and maintained a summer residence tucked away from the shoreline. When folks hiked through and across the dunes, they knew they were trespassing, but they skirted the Denison cottage and honored the habitat where migrating birds often paused on their travels. They cherished the landscape and respected the lost town of Singapore.

In 1998, the Michigan Department of Natural Resources sought to buy the four hundred and twenty acres so they could link it to the Saugatuck Dunes State Park, and the City of Saugatuck petitioned to annex a section to their Oval Beach. While elderly Mr. Denison wanted his land to remain a protected nature preserve, his children argued with him. After Mr. Denison died, the land could not be sold until the lawyers untangled issues within the estate. But in 2006, McClendon paid the Denison heirs 39.5 million dollars for the four hundred acres. Like the investors who created Singapore, McClendon saw wealth hidden in the dunes. He would build a gated resort with a marina, riding stables, a shooting range and multi-million-dollar cottages, but he did not know the history buried beneath the sand.

Police lined the walls of the Saugatuck High School room, where a hundred grim residents filled rows of metal folding chairs. They wore denim and Carhartt work clothing and snow dripped from their boots and shoes. The police glanced at a small sign noting the room's fire code capacity and counted heads. Many of our friends sat near my husband and me, and our rage rose like a waterspout twisting off Lake Michigan. Great Lakes water ran in the veins of the artists, writers, teachers, farmers, and shop owners. We were determined to fight for those sacred dunes with passion and creativity.

McClendon's lawyer pointed to maps, outlining the proposed development and how much tax revenue it would bring to Saugatuck. We muttered; a few friends softly swore. McClendon's lawyer might predict future incomes, but he had not researched the local demographics who disapproved of his development. Nor had he considered the current sums spent by visitors who came to Oval Beach and would not want to look at a gated community.

One by one, people drifted to the microphone and begged the zoning commission not to rezone the Denison acreage for development. One young man read a letter from a soldier serving in Afghanistan who recounted how hiking through the dunes sustained his inner peace. He yearned to return from his deployment and find the land preserved.

Behind us, a friend nudged a gray-haired man. "You're a judge. Speak up. You know Michigan's environmental laws." He shook his head as a couple of men wrote on a yellow legal pad. "Those local guys are lawyers and are organizing free legal counsel."

At the end of the evening, the zoning commission allowed the variance, so the Saugatuck Dunes Coastal Alliance formed. While the locals could not stop the development, they would litigate and whittle away McClendon's plans to ravage the dunes.

An artist friend, her husband, and her six-year-old daughter hosted a benefit for the Alliance at their home. Young Rose sold notecards she painted, and her mother displayed small watercolors for sale. On the kitchen counter, checks and large bills filled a basket for donations. The leader of the Alliance, David Swan, explained that the Land Conservancy of West Michigan had discovered several endangered plants growing on a certain portion of the dunes and had alerted the zoning commission about them.

"We will buy this land. Inch by inch, we will thwart McClendon," David announced.

The State of Michigan recognized the endangered species growing on the 173 acres south of the Kalamazoo River, making it worthless to McClendon. He sold it for nineteen million dollars to a coalition composed of the Land Conservancy, conservationists, local organizations, and citizens who gave the land to Saugatuck. The newly preserved Saugatuck Harbor Natural Area opened to walkers. But when their feet reached the McClendon property, security cameras recorded them stepping into the water in order to avoid trespassing as they strolled down the shore.

While cooking dinner on a mild spring evening and listening to the radio, the journalist on All Things Considered reported, "On March 1st, the U. S. Department of Justice's Antitrust Division filed criminal charges against Aubrey McClendon, alleging that he and an unnamed company agreed not to bid against each other on drilling leases. Today, McClendon died when his car smashed into the cement wall supporting an overpass bridge."

I closed my eyes. While I hated what McClendon had represented, I prayed for his wife and three children and the maze of emotion his family now wandered. What would become of the Denison property?

Years passed until another investor bought the land from the McClendon estate. He also proposed a gated development that included dredging a channel for a marina. He ignored the necessary permits required by the state and hauled in bulldozers, shoving the sand into roads. But the Alliance sued, demanding that construction stop until the permits were applied for, reviewed, and issued. Court battle after battle continued while winds whipped the sand into dust devils.

Under a sapphire sky, I ambled up the hill leading to Miss Bartow's cottage, now owned by a descendant of the first families, who created this special place called the Knolls. My clogs clomped down the wooden stairs leading to the beach, but the stairs ended a few feet off the ground. I leapt, sinking into the sand. For over thirty years, I've sat on this dune, filling my soul with the movement and sound of the waves, watching how wind and water carve the sand. With my parents, I traveled to all the Great Lakes, but Miss Bartow gave me her love of this place on Lake Michigan.

Like the Irish, my mentor understood the concept of duchas, that our souls can find a natural affinity for a place. Although Miss Bartow dwelled nine months amidst the cornfields of central Illinois, her spirit embraced this dune as her true home. Beneath tall red oak trees, her rustic cottage blended into the landscape where in the spring, hundreds of Dutchman Britches and Jack-in-the-Pulpit bloomed. She cherished the history of the Native Americans whose feet dented the depression into the Bear Path. And she told tales of how the lakeshore affected animals, like the family from Chicago who brought their dingy white cat to their summer cottage. The cat looked at the lake and washed away the city soot until it shone like a pearl.

Miss Bartow loved the wildness of these dunes. In her last few years, she rolled her wheelchair onto the sun porch and sustained her crumbling body with a view she had revered for over eight decades. When her final days arrived, Miss Bartow lay on a hospital bed positioned near the bank of windows, breathing in the roar of the waves and the amber sunset turning Lake Michigan gold.

I dumped most of the sand out of my clogs, but some grains clung to my toes. I retreated up the stairs. The wind and the waves whispered, stirring my soul and scattering the sand.

Works Cited

Ashcroft, Brent. "Buried Singapore: Remnants of lost village are hiding in plain sight." WZZM 13 News [Grand Rapids, MI], 12 Feb. 2019. https://www.wzzm13.com/article/news/local/michigan-life/remnants-of-buried-singapore-are-hiding-in-plain-sight-today/69-51227c66-54b9-4164-8c97-e090891a1318

Bruley, Bryan, Joe Carroll, and Ashlyn Loder. "The Incredible Rise and Final Hours of Fracking King Aubrey McClendon." Bloomberg Business, 10 March 2016. https://www.bloomberg.com/features/2016-aubrey-mcclendon/

O'Connell, Patrick. "The story of 'Michigan's Pompeii': How the small town of Singapore was forgotten beneath the sand." The Chicago Tribune, 21 Nov. 2020. https://www.chicagotribune.com/news/environment/great-lakes/ct-lake-michigan-climate-change-buried-town-singapore-20201120-zn2kxnv4d5a3jkrue7dvphog4q-htmlstory.html

Resources

https://www.chicagotribune.com/news/environment/great-lakes/ct-lake-michigan-climate-change-buried-town-singapore-20201120-zn2kxnv4d5a3jkrue7dvphog4q-htmlstory.html

https://www.wzzm13.com/article/news/local/michigan-life/remnants-of-buried-singapore-are-hiding-in-plain-sight-today/69-51227c66-54b9-4164-8c97-e090891a1318

The Incredible Rise and Final Hours of Fracking King Aubrey McClendon, Bloomberg Business. March 10, 2016

Nathan Eckstein
TEXTS ON A DELAYED AMTRAK

: hey guess whose train is stopped

A couple is missing a funeral.
Feign sleep, peer out muddied glass,
side-eye a new passenger if only to say
these stretched legs cannot share.

: it's been 3 hrs hah

Confuse fumes for sky as if all this grey
spouts from the same abused smokestacks
of American Steel to obscure distractions –
or shores I'll just once shutter stop past.

: i can call?

Describe Erie frozen? Accompany me
across this expanse, stillness, this ice over.
Turn to leftward horizons, its soiled cousins –
American Farm lying wan, torpid and unthawed.

: you must be in class

Let's walk these waters. Ice wants to break
like us fractured, cracked open.
Talk to me and rupture this frigid rest,
these broken waves but
You know not to say

anything –
So I won't bluster,   screech.

: nvm
: gonna sleep

I want to drift as Amtrak twitches through
side to side to side to side rocking away from stuck
to drifting because late or not prostrate or not
we hurtle forward.

Laura Ross
I WAS RENOVATING AN OLD DOLLHOUSE
WHEN YOU WALKED OUT

By the time you left,
I had already taken out the staircase,
removed the railing from the balcony's edge.
In the days I waited to hear from you,
I salvaged wood floors and kitchen cabinets,
snapped moldings from yellowed glue.
I chose coral-pink for the house.
It had to be the favorite color of mermaids
and those who are free to be whimsical.
      Did I need the weathervane?
            The atmosphere, unsettled.
I flowered window boxes, hung a beaded chandelier
over the clawfoot tub, painted the shutters Caribbean blue.
The week of my birthday, small packages began to arrive —
      a basket of peaches, a ginger jar,
      a sunburst mirror, soft roses in resin.
            No word from you.

Like any dreamer, I cozied myself inside rooms
where tiny books didn't open, and lamps didn't shine.
The word *love*, a clever pattern of repetition
            on wallpaper in a room meant for a girl
in a house where nothing could change unless I wanted it to.
The hedge, thick, green, and precise.
Lemons arranged in a blue and white bowl.
Did I mention the front door can never be locked?
That your wedding band, when traced, is the size of a platter.
That there are things I can't change
            and things that I can —
Pot of tea, loaf of bread.
      Towels rolled in a leather trimmed basket.
      Roman shades in the bay window.
Where to put the orange tree and the easel.

Alex Carrigan
RACING INTO THE NIGHT
After Yoasobi

We were dissolving, you and me, skies above and wide,
racing into a true night with only a goodbye.

> Only a goodbye is implied to those who come across the scene,
> wondering if it was easy to keep our hands together in the air.

In the air, you covered my eyes and I covered yours,
as if we were playing Blindman's Bluff like when we were children.

> When we were children, we thought we would eventually see all
> of the world together, experiences and memories were all we shared.

All we shared when we finally grew up were pleas and tears,
making it hard to see anything beyond the horizon from up on the roof.

> Up on the roof, I finally understood why you kept
> calling me there no matter how many times I pulled you down.

You pulled me down too, and from the ground I can see
we are dissolving, you and me, skies above and wide.

Laura Ross
GRIEF FROM A BIRD'S EYE VIEW

Sometimes I'll zoom in close enough to see
Domenica, Bonaire, St. Lucia, Eleuthera —
islands that read off the blue map
like sun glittered confections. An archipelago
of rum and hummingbirds; you and me

in our tender burning skin. Moving closer,
Florida becomes a shimmering column of green
with foam edges and inland springs so clear
we watch our shadows glide across sand floors.

Do you see the roof of our house on the lake?
A son and a daughter and an aqua pool. Ospreys
nesting in mossy cypress and a moon that floats up
from the same point on the horizon as space coast rockets.

From this perspective, I could witness hurricanes
and wildfires, and the lightning strike that took out
an oak while grounding itself in the tire swing.
Headlights sigh past the window in our bedroom,
the night lit with jasmine you planted two autumns ago.
Its tendrils lace the arbor where your pin nails hold.
There's a tiny scar on the knuckle of your forefinger.
Ambers eclipsed by the pupil of your eye.

I see myself there, and I look closer at what I am
holding. It's bird we tried to rescue years ago —
a fuzzy hatchling with matchstick bones,
and when its quickened heart lost its hunger,
we told the children it flew away, and they believed us,
because why wouldn't they? Why wouldn't they

believe that grief perches on a high branch
and sings with fevered eyes. That it lofts over
fence lines and treetops and the detours of highways
where your truck rolls on silently without a radio.

From these heights, there isn't much to hear anyway.
What was promised or implored is garbled in wind.
The horizon scrolling forward. Clouds,
an essence of neither sweetness nor regret.

Ken Been
MY FATHER

I picture us working a midnight shift
holding in the between of our thumb and forefinger
the truth of a seven-sixteenths

just off the perfection of the halves we`d share at 4 a.m. lunch
apples and sandwiches
a king's feast under the lunch pail moon

then off we go to twist the axis of the world, spinning
time clockwise with a crescent wrench
tightening our days and nights

turn by turn
the grabbing thread attaching dimensions for me
with the forever in his old, metal tool box.

Joy Gaines-Friedler
COMMUNION

3/28/90: I'm injecting Interferon in my stomach — taking the pills
and DDI — Jesus what an array.   —James Kerr

Our last conversation, you said,
that all your life   you'd been a *shadow.*
Then you said,
          it is time for this to end
and shocked me
          with   *pray for me.*
I thought of our ritual of passing around the bong
on Sunday mornings, how you called it
          Morning Mass,
and the Communion I took
while attending church with you one day
     surprised by the way the wafer melted in my mouth
before I returned to kneel next to your laughing shoulders,
  your eyes a bit scared for my brazen Jewish soul.
Before you slipped away from me
                    I wanted to remind you
how fun it was to slide Kahlua into our coffee,
dance to "Stairway to Heaven," stay up all night
talking about God and fathers   —how, despite the lesions
and new words, like *lesions,*
                    and *pneumatoid,*
I will always feel the stone warmth of you.
I am glad that your death eyes were 3000 miles away,
that it was your mother who was there to look into them,
telling you to let go,
          and I am sorry that it was not me.
I'm thinking,
maybe I will lie and say that
          I held the hand of my best friend as he died from AIDS,
          which I do — only, it isn't a lie.

Jennifer Patino
THE LAKE STURGEON

we stumbled upon the sturgeon release
on the Boardman-Ottaway
and my moth-eaten ribbon skirt
caught tears of resiliency

they say a female nmé can live 150 years,
a male 80, and there's hundreds
of young fish in red plastic buckets
impatient for open water, yearning to mature

an elder sings a medicine song
to guide him along and upriver
an earth drum directs the flow
of rebalance, of rejuvenation

I watch him swim a silent prayer
for my people to always remember
the currents that connect us,
the streams, like us, that are still here

Alison Swan
NONE OF THIS ENDS

I see the way your feet are shaped by ground
       your fingertips by bark
and your limbs by the bend of branches.

      You already know so many hues if you name
and record for a hundred years you'll make
      only a partial list of what you know.

I see the way you have climbed into the crown
      then retreated to the lowest crook.
What fearlessness made you let go?

      You must have been looking skyward
because you landed flat on your back and Earth
      knocked air from your lungs.

The house's back door was
      a million miles away. Your mother and grandmother
were visiting past three doors.

      You lay still and focused on breath, smelled
grass and ground ivy.
      Earth cushioned you, head to feet.

Alison Swan
RETURNING TO EARTH

A buff-gray cardinal
        tipped orange
                strikes the soaked snag of
    a little tree I cut
  back hard
One high note
    cricketing becomes from
                a distance
        might be the
  sound of leaves drying
Across the roadway
        fields blare among
                felled shadows and
            clipped bits
    Why not allow this
mallet to craze
        my shell
            She sings
    I'm telling you
She sings

Kathleen McGookey

PICK ANY SUMMER DAY,

then resurrect one detail—girl running with a butterfly net, the soft ache of the sky after sunset, boy digging a hole on the beach—before everything slips away. It's been years since I tended grief like a small, fierce pet, smoothing its fur in prayer. Today, the invisible harp plays bird calls like a brown thrasher at the top of a pine, cycling through a smacking kiss, a slurred whistle, then an almost-human voice calling *bury it, bury it, bury it* —

William Palmer
THE BOULDER
Grand Traverse Bay, Michigan

The boulder is straight out
    from the birch on the hill,
        though rarely

do I find it.
    When I do,
        I glimpse it

just under
    the green hue of a wave,
        a white-rose heap

of granite thousands of years old
    set in soft sand.
        I rub its coarse surface,

perch myself on it,
    inhale the smell
        of warm wind,

then crouch
    holding on
        eye-level —

rollers
    rushing over
        my shoulders.

Russ Thorburn
WALT WHITMAN AND HIS LAKE SUPERIOR BAPTISM

Memory mixes in with the first chill of the water.
He looks upon that blue of Lake Superior
like a mother's apron, and uses its clarity
to cleanse himself, direct his hand to point
toward a ledge of rock named Ripley.
The Civil War remains behind him with
his rucksack of journals, the words stripped.
Whitman peers down at his toes moving
over the sand underwater, its mirror
reflects his overweight body.
He fits his belly into this baptism,
allowing the cold to touch his knees, bruised
hips next, forcing his living breath
to meet the waves with his watery kiss.

Joanne Esser
WHERE I'M FROM

I first belonged to Lake Michigan,
to its cold gray waves, sharp whitecaps,
its terrible, changeable moods
and how it crashes against the rocks
I once climbed on. The never-still voice
of wind, its power over water — thrilling,
a little bit frightening.

But also to its splinters of silver, lilting notes
lifted on the tips of splash. White-bright
sun reflected in shards. Vast glistening.
Both at once.

Was I born in awe?
I rose there, a girl brought so often
to the cusp of something.

A birthplace to which I keep returning
as if called by that shifting gleam.
Child of water, light, ice. Standing near
but rarely entering its chill, its grip.
Slippery boundary. I hold my breath,
balance there on the flat tops of boulders,
chips of solid earth piled at its edge.
So many days spent poised on the brink
of land and lake, working to keep equilibrium.

Linda Nemec Foster
A YEAR, A DAY, THE SPIRIT OF THE LAKE

I.   Spring, Sunrise, A Language That Sings

From the mouth of the river
to the foot of the dunes,
from Oval Beach and its waves
to Baldhead and its wind,
the day rises as spring awakens.
The sun kisses every cloud, every
hint of blue as it beckons each rose
to blossom, each robin to leave its nest.
A little boy and a little girl open
their eyes to the new day and never
blink. Constant movement, constant flow.
From the sparkling edge of the blue water
to the top of the highest dune, the children
know both worlds. They invent a language that sings.

II.   Summer, Afternoon, A Necklace of Light

In her youth, her wonder-filled youth,
the full sun of summer.
Endless days as the light
dances on the waves
with the sheer brilliance
of diamonds. The young woman
watches the reflections all day
as the lake's shining waters
flow from thin horizon
to wide embrace of beach.
As if she could weave that
brilliance into a necklace
of light: iridescent shine that
would never dim, never die.

III.   Fall, Sunset, The Sound of Wings on Water

In his middle years, his quiet middle years,
the man walks the shore
and seeks the glowing
sunset on the waters.
The colors of autumn
alive on the waves:
crimson, orange, deep, deep
gold. But it's the sound
of the gulls that fill him
with amazement. How their gray
wings touch the water
with such grace, they
sound like paper unfolding —
an unread letter to his heart.

IV.   Winter, Night, The Song of the Moon

From the mouth of the river
to the foot of the dunes,
from Oval Beach and its waves
to Baldhead and its wind,
the night descends as winter dreams.
Tonight, the moon is a crescent —
a hint of silver, veiled in mist.
It sings a low melody that pulses
in each wave, in each heartbeat
of the eldest, the wise: those men
and women alive with the most memories.
They provide the lyrics to the song
the moon sings over and over again
as it reaches the shore, as it reaches the shore.

Commissioned by The Lakeshore Community Chorus, Douglas, Michigan, in celebration of its fifteenth anniversary.

Jerry Dennis
THREE BRIEF PROSE PIECES

ME V. WINTER (1)

This morning I pulled snow from the roof with my long-handled rake and had to be careful not to pull the house down with it.

Started clearing the driveway with the snowblower but the auger jammed on a block of ice and something inside the gearbox shrieked expensively. Got a wrench and opened it and found it packed with chrome confetti.

Traded the blower for a shovel and dug a tunnel to the mailbox but froze when my hand touched the mailbox handle. What if somebody had booby-trapped it? I eased the door open just a crack and, sure enough, a scarlet tanager shoved past me, burst through the roof of my tunnel, and resumed its migration south.

Went inside the house and sat by the fireplace watching fire shimmy up the chimney after being trapped inside wood for a hundred years. The fireplace is greedy. It eats pieces of trees like popcorn. Its favorites in order of preference are maple, beech, butternut, bone. Ironwood it spits out in disgust. Maybe ironwood's an acquired taste. All I know is I can't split the stuff. When I try, my ax handle shatters and the head flies away end over end and disappears in the snow. No matter how hard I search I won't find it until spring.

HALF MOON, IRON JAW

Lately I've been thinking about missed opportunities. Not fishing with Steve, for instance, in the ponds near his cabin south of Munising that are full of bluegills and bass and have poetry in their names: Red Jack, Blue Joe, Half Moon, Iron Jaw. He invited me to visit in September, when the mosquitoes are gone and it's the best time to fish during the day and watch the northern lights at night.

Instead, I stayed home and worked. Cranked out a magazine article on a subject I've forgotten and a few pages of a memoir I'll probably never finish titled Upstream All the Way. My friend Kelly says he knows what they'll inscribe on my headstone: "At Least He Got a Lot of Work Done."

Last night Steve phoned to say he sold his cabin. A billionaire who's been buying whole sections of Upper Peninsula forest, clear-cutting the trees for pulp and parceling the denuded land into vacation lots for downstaters, bought it along with Half Moon, Iron Jaw, and the others. Rumor is he plans to run cables under the ponds, harness them to a fleet of transport helicopters, and airlift them hundreds of miles south to a gated property he's developing near Winnetka called Buena Vista Hills. He'll change their names to Uno, Dos, Tres, Cuatro, then poison the bass and bluegills and replace them with genetically engineered rainbow trout that grow twenty inches a year, leap on command for their photos to be taken, and can be caught only with artificial flies sold exclusively to club members for a hundred dollars each. "It's a bargain!" the investors will shout while lounging beside the infinity pool, pounding tequila handcrafted by movie stars, and discussing the majestic redwoods of California. All that top-dollar timber just standing there: what a waste.

ME V. WINTER (2)

With the last of my retirement savings, I bought a powerful new snowblower named My Blue Ox and put it to work clearing drifts from last night's storm.

I'd like to say the drifts were as big as condominiums, but they were only as big as duplexes. According to my state-of-the-art weather apparatus, the temperature was 51 degrees below zero and the wind was gusting to 82 mph, but that was nothing to me and My Blue Ox. We ripped through the drifts and shot them in a firehose jet five miles across East Bay. Sorry, Elk Rapids.

My neighbor wandered over and asked if we could help with his driveway too. "Sure thing, Chief!" said My Blue Ox, and we made short work of it.

Then the governor called to say that hundreds of children were trapped inside the elementary school with their young teachers and were desperate for pancakes and a presence of strong encouragement. My Blue Ox and I rushed to their aid and fixed things up pretty quick. Oh, the world is strange and filled with wonders and I don't mind getting old at all.

CONTRIBUTOR BIOS

*CATHERINE ANDERSON's most recent book is *My Brother Speaks in Dreams: Of Family, Beauty & Belonging*, a memoir about her Michigan childhood with her late brother Charlie. She's published four full-length collections of poems and lives in Kansas City, MO where she worked with new refugees and immigrants for 21 years.

*KEN BEEN's poetry has been published or is forthcoming in numerous journals internationally. Recent placements include *The Brussels Review, The Primer, LIT Magazine, The Opiate, Aethlon, Dodging The Rain, New Feathers Anthology* and *The RavensPerch*. His work also can be found in many other fine publications. He is from Detroit.

GENEVIEVE BETTS is the author of *A New Kind of Tongue* (FlowerSong Press, 2023) and *An Unwalled City* (Prolific Press, 2015). Her work has appeared in a variety of journals and anthologies. She is an assistant professor at Santa Fe Community College and teaches for Arcadia University's low-residency MFA program.

ALEX CARRIGAN (he/him) is a Pushcart-nominated editor, poet, and critic from Alexandria, VA. He is the author of *Now Let's Get Brunch: A Collection of RuPaul's Drag Race Twitter Poetry* (Querencia Press, 2023).

*JUDY CHILDS taught ELA for twenty years in Traverse City's East Middle School's 8th grade, entertaining and learning with her students. Bringing in her love of nature, hiking, and traveling, she shared her heart with her students. She is now an enthusiastic member of Interlochen's Summer Writers Retreat.

*CHRIS COCHRAN is a high school English teacher who writes first drafts on an old typewriter in a small nook beneath his basement steps. His work has appeared in *The 2024 Northwind Treasury* and the *Write Michigan 2023* Anthology. He lives in Michigan with his wife and son.

*JERRY DENNIS's many books include *The Living Great Lakes* and *Up North in Michigan*. His poetry and prose have appeared in *PANK, Mid-American Review, Michigan Quarterly Review, New World Writing, Abandon Journal,* and many other places. He lives in northern Michigan.

*JOAN DONALDSON was ten when she glued paper onto a piece of cardboard and listed the birds she saw that year. Now, she walks around her organic farm, observing changes in plants and listening to birds. Black Rose Writing will release her latest novel, *Ae Fond Kiss*, in January 2025.

114

NATHAN ECKSTEIN was born in Chicago. He works and lives abroad.

JOANNE ESSER is author of the poetry collection *Humming At The Dinner Table*, the chapbook *I Have Always Wanted Lightning*, and the recently released *All We Can Do Is Name Them* (Fernwood Press, 2024). She earned an MFA from Hamline University and has been a teacher of young children for over forty years.

PAULA FERNANDEZ lives in Illinois where she writes poems from a bench looking out over Lake Michigan. She grew up in rural Oklahoma, the daughter of a farmhand and a mystic. Her poetry often grapples with the simple but difficult question, "Where are you from?" This is her debut publication.

*LINDA NEMEC FOSTER has published 14 collections of poetry including her most recent book, *The Lake Huron Mermaid* (with Anne-Marie Oomen and Meridith Ridl). Foster's collection of prose poems, *Bone Country*, was honored as a Distinguished Favorite in NYC's Big Book Award in Poetry for 2024.

*JOY GAINES-FRIEDLER is the author of four books of poetry. Her chapbook *Stone on Your Stone* was co-winner of the Celery City Chapbook Prize. Joy is currently teaching, pro bono, for KickstART Farmington. She is also teaching private Creative Writing workshops. A fifth book, *Secular Audacity*, is forthcoming in 2025.

KIMBERLY GIBSON-TRAN has poems and essays appearing or forthcoming in *Reed Magazine, Rowayat, Jelly Squid, Saranac Review, Paper Dragon, Thin Air Magazine, Sheepshead Review, Saw Palm, Pandan Weekly, RockPaperPoem, Anodyne Magazine,* and *Elysium Review.* Raised by medical missionaries in Thailand, she now lives in Princeton, Texas.

*MARY JO FIRTH GILLETT's collection, *Soluble Fish*, won the Crab Orchard First Book Contest. Four award-winning chapbooks have also been published. Poems have appeared in *The Southern Review, New Ohio Review, Plant-Human Quarterly, Southern Poetry Review, Dunes Review, Poetry Daily, Verse Daily,* and elsewhere.

*BRYAN GRULEY is a novelist and journalist who shared in *The Wall Street Journal's* Pulitzer Prize for coverage of 9/11. His sixth novel, *Bitterfrost*, set in a fictional northern Michigan town, will be published in April. He lives in Traverse City with his wife, Pam.

CAITLIN ANNETTE JOHNSON is a backwoods, Mississippi-raised hayseed turned Queens-based queer with a kid and a dog. She received MFA from Syracuse University. She is a proud member of her local PTA's Library Committee and hosts a free weekly poetry workshop in her community.

JULIA LEWIS is continually fascinated by the intersection of writing and education, spurring a career that weaves between the two. From the classroom to museum exhibitions and narrative podcasts, she has spent her time exploring these two lifelong loves. She lives in Indianapolis with her husband, daughter, and six cats.

*ELLEN LORD's poetry is nestled in anthologies including: *Bear River Writers Review, Contemporary Haibun Online, Drifting Sands, Frogpond, Failed Haiku, Peninsula Poets, Yooper Poetry, U.P. Reader*, and *Walloon Writers Review*. She resides in Charlevoix County and Trout Creek, Michigan. Her chapbook, *Relative Sanity* (2023) is available at ellenlordauthor.com.

*DR. MAESTRO (MD, MBA) is a retired physician living in Oscoda, Michigan. Dr. Maestro has self-published three books: *Leadership Lessons From History* (2016), *Deconstructing Genesis* (2024), and *Deconstructing Exodus* (2025). Dr. Maestro is a member of the Oscoda Writer's Group.

*KATHLEEN MCGOOKEY has published five books and four chapbooks, most recently *Cloud Reports* (Celery City Chapbooks) and *Paper Sky* (Press 53). Her work has appeared in journals including *Copper Nickel, Epoch, Glassworks, Hunger Mountain, Los Angeles Review, North American Review*, and *The Southern Review*.

ZACH KEALI'I MURPHY is a Hawaii-born writer with a background in cinema. His stories appear in *The MacGuffin, Reed Magazine, The Coachella Review, Raritan Quarterly, Another Chicago Magazine*, and more. He published the chapbook *Tiny Universes* (Selcouth Station Press). He lives with his wonderful wife, Kelly, in St. Paul, Minnesota.

*WILLIAM PALMER's poetry has appeared in *Ecotone, JAMA, One Art,* and other journals. He is the author of two chapbooks: *A String of Blue Lights* and *Humble,* and *Discovering Arguments: An Introduction to Critical Thinking, Writing, and Style*. A retired professor of English at Alma College, he lives in Traverse City, Michigan.

*JENNIFER PATINO is a poet residing in Traverse City, Michigan who adores books and film. She is an enrolled member of the Lac Courte Oreilles Band of Lake Superior Ojibwe.

JARED PEARCE grew up in California and now lives in Iowa. His poetry collections include *Down Their Spears* and *The Annotated Murder of One*. Website: https://jaredpearcepoetry.weebly.com.

*ERICA PHOTIADES is from Royal Oak, Michigan. She is a professional violinist and orchestra teacher. Her writing has been featured on the NoSleep Podcast and won the 2024 New Mexico Department of Cultural Affairs Ekphrastic Poetry Contest. She is the author of *Lightbearer*. She lives in Albuquerque, New Mexico.

JOHN RANDALL has been a trash collector, a copy editor, and an attorney. He likes firewood, the sky, and the First Amendment. His poetry has appeared in *Atlanta Review, DMQ Review,* and *Florida Review.* He is a Pushcart Prize and Best of the Net nominee. Online he is johnbrandall.com.

*CHRISTINE RHEIN is the author of *Wild Flight* (Walt McDonald Book Prize, Texas Tech University Press). Her poems have appeared in *The Southern Review, Michigan Quarterly Review,* and *Rattle,* and in many anthologies, including *The Best American Nonrequired Reading.* A former automotive engineer, Christine lives in Brighton, Michigan.

*JOAN GALLAGHER RICHMOND, a graduate of the Art Academy of Cincinnati and holding an MFA from the University of Notre Dame, taught painting at Northwestern Michigan College and continues to instruct workshops. Richmond works both in plein air and in studio. See joanrichmondart.com.

LAURA SOBBOTT ROSS has worked as a teacher and a writing coach for Lake County Schools in Central Florida and was named Lake County's poet laureate. She is the author of two poetry chapbooks and three full-length poetry books.

HANNAH ROWELL is a graduate of Bowling Green State University. Fate located her in Ohio against her will, though she's uncertain where she would rather be. She would prefer you envision her as being a palm-sized gastropod. Her work can be found in *Mythulu, In Parentheses, Pumpernickel House,* and elsewhere.

KAYLEE J. SCHOFIELD lives by a decommissioned nuclear power plant with her partner, three pets, and a host of harmless spiders. Her poetry has appeared in *Wild Roof Journal, La Piccioletta Barca*, and others. She was a finalist for the 2022 Honeybee Prize in Fiction.

LEAH SKAY is an emerging author from Delaware. She received her B.A. in Writing from Ithaca College and has published fiction, nonfiction, and poetry across the internet and print publications of the U.S.A and beyond, including *Sunspot Lit, Iron Horse Literary Review*, and more.

*ONNA SOLOMON's first full-length poetry manuscript is a semi-finalist for the 2024 Yesyes Books Pamet River Prize. Her writing has appeared in *Hobart, Denver Quarterly,* and *32 Poems,* among others. Her poem "Autism Suite" was awarded the Beloit Poetry Journal's Chad Walsh Poetry Prize. She lives in Ann Arbor, MI.

*NANCY SQUIRES' writing has appeared in *Dunes Review, Blueline Magazine, Split Rock Review*, and *Writers Resist*. In 2014 she self-published a memoir, *The Cottage: Portrait of a Place*, set on the shores of Grand Traverse Bay. She lives in Michigan with her partner and two cats.

*PHILLIP STERLING's most recent book is *Lessons in Geography: The Education of a Michigan Poet*. His works of fiction include *In Which Brief Stories Are Told, Amateur Husbandry*, and stories in Best Short Fiction 2017 and Best Microfiction 2024.

*ALISON SWAN was born in Detroit. She has authored several books, including *A Fine Canopy* which was shortlisted for a Poetry Medal from Independent Publisher (IPPY), and highly recommended by *Orion* and *LitHub*. She has new work forthcoming in *Third Coast, Crab Orchard Review*, and others.

*RUSSELL THORBURN was the first poet laureate of the Upper Peninsula. *Let It Be Told in a Single Breath* and the forthcoming *And the Heart Will Not Quicken* are published by Cornerstone Press, University of Wisconsin, Stevens Point. Both collections use titles taken from the poetry of William Everson.

*CALVIN VANERGENS is a Michigan poet whose work has appeared at *Ekstasis, The Tiger Moth Review, Reformed Journal, The Purpled Nail*, and *Cantos*.

ESTHER CAROL HALEY WALKER grew up near the rolling foothills of Virginia's Blue Ridge Mountains. She is a graduate of Harvard Law School and the University of Virginia. She lives in New Hampshire with her family. Her short stories have been published in *The Virginia Literary Review, Rathalla Review*, and at Sleetmagazine.com.

JOHN WALSER's poems have appeared in numerous journals, including *Spillway, Water-Stone Review, Plume, Posit* and *december magazine*. A four-time semifinalist for the Pablo Neruda Prize and a two-time Pushcart nominee, John is a professor of English at Marian University and lives in Fond du Lac, Wisconsin, with his wife, Julie.

MELINDA WOLF is a clinical social worker who works providing therapy to veterans. Her poetry has been published in the journals *American Literary Review, New York Quarterly*, and *Mudfish*, among others. Big Wonderful Press published her chapbook *There is a Greeting As Well As a Parting* in 2017.

*JANICE ZERFAS lives near Eau Claire, Michigan, site of orchards and migrant workers; browsing deer and beloved passed-on ghosts; home and loss. She has poems in *South Dakota Review, Rattle*, and more. She was teacher of the year once upon a time, and now, retired, she can write until midnight!

STAFF BIOS

*KELLI FITZPATRICK is an author, editor, and teacher from Michigan. Her first novel, *Captain Marvel: Carol Danvers Declassified*, releases in 2025. Her short fiction has been published by Simon and Schuster, Flash Fiction Online, and others. She has edited for Modiphius Entertainment and the *Journal of Popular Culture*. Website: KelliFitzpatrick.com

*CHRIS GIROUX received his doctorate from Wayne State University and is a professor of English at Saginaw Valley State University, where he has served as faculty advisor for the school's literary magazine and co-founded the community arts journal *Still Life*. His second chapbook, *Sheltered in Place*, was released in 2022.

*ANNE-MARIE OOMEN is Michigan Author for 2023-24. Her memoir, *As Long As I Know You: The Mom Book* won AWP's Sue William Silverman Nonfiction Award. She wrote *Lake Michigan Mermaid* with Linda Nemec Foster, *Love, Sex and 4-H* (Next Generation Indie Award/Memoir), and others. *The Lake Huron Mermaid* is most recent, now out.

*JOHN MAUK has published a range of stories and nonfiction works, including his full collections, *Field Notes for the Earthbound* and *Where All Things Flatten.* John also hosts Prose from the Underground, a YouTube video series for working writers. For more information, see johnmauk.com.

*SARA MAURER writes in Sault Ste. Marie, Michigan. Place deeply informs her writing. Her work has appeared in *Hominum Journal, Dunes Review, The Twin Bill,* and others. She was a 2023 Suzanne Wilson Artist-in-Residence at Glen Arbor Art Center. Her debut novel is forthcoming in Winter 2026 from St. Martin's Press.

*TERESA SCOLLON recently published *Trees and Other Creatures* (Alice Greene). A National Endowment for the Arts fellow, she teaches the Writers Studio program at North Ed Career Tech in Traverse City. Her fourth poetry collection, *No Trouble Staying Awake,* is forthcoming from Cornerstone Press in April 2025.

*YVONNE STEPHENS is a poet, rural librarian, amateur mycologist and mental health activist. *The Salt Before It Shakes* was published by Hidden Timber Books in 2017. Her work has appeared in *Dunes Review, Family Stories from the Attic, Eucalypt,* and *iō Literary Journal*.

*JENNIFER YEATTS' literary life has included MA and MFA degrees in poetry, teaching writing in various forms, a handful of small publications, and editorial roles at *Passages North* and *Fugue*. She works as an educator for Higher Grounds Coffee (www.coffeelearninglab.com).

SUBMISSION GUIDELINES

Dunes Review welcomes work from writers at all stages of their careers living anywhere in the world, though we particularly love featuring those with ties to Michigan and the Midwest. We are open to all styles and aesthetics, but please read the following carefully to dive a little deeper into what we're looking for.

Ultimately, we're looking for work that draws us in from the very first line: with image, with sound, with sense, with lack of sense. We're looking for writing that makes us *feel* and bowls us over, lifts us up, and takes us places we've never been to show us ordinary things in ways we've never seen them. We're looking for poems and stories and essays that teach us how to read them and pull us back to their beginnings as soon as we've read their final lines. We're looking for things we can't wait to read again, things we can't resist sharing with the nearest person who will listen. Send us your best work. We'll give it our best attention.

Submissions are accepted only via our Submittable platform: www.dunesreview.submittable.com. We do not consider work sent through postal mail or email. Any submissions sent through email will not be read or responded to. Please see further guidelines posted on our site. We look forward to reading your work!

www.ingramcontent.com/pod-product-compliance
Lightning Source LLC
Chambersburg PA
CBHW031724150125
20230CB00005B/15